The Secret Recipes of an *Overcomer*

"How to transition from Defeat to Victory"

ARLETHA KENT
7 LITERARY COLLABORATORS

The Secret Recipes of an Overcomer. How to Transition from Defeat to Victory.

Please direct all copyright inquiries to:
The Literary Lighthouse Alliance
8951 Cypress Waters Blvd., Suite 160
Coppell, TX 75019

Paperback ISBN: 979-8-218-35851-8

Layout & Design: The Literary Lighthouse Alliance Publishing

Printed in the United States.

DEDICATION

In this book, I pour my heart out in dedication to the man who was not just a mentor but a Pastor and spiritual father to me – Elder Earnest Jackson, who now resides with the Lord. I am humbled by the lessons he instilled in me, teaching me to battle in the spirit with God's divine Word and persist without ever backing down!

My gratitude for Pastor Jackson's life and ministry can't be expressed in words. He shaped my life in ways I never anticipated, leaving an indelible mark on my life's journey. His profound knowledge and wisdom will continue to be a compass for me as I embark upon my many aspirations and endeavors.

It's my deepest desire that this book will resonate with all of you, igniting a spark of encouragement for those on the quest for spiritual growth and renewal. I truly believe we all can learn from Pastor Jackson's remarkable legacy of faith!

So, as you turn these pages, I hope you can feel the love and dedication that went into every word. Thank you for inviting this book into your life and may the grace and peace of God touch your soul in the most unexpected ways. Here's to Elder Earnest Jackson, a shining example of unwavering faith.
Happy reading, and God bless!

ACKNOWLEDGEMENT

While birthing The Secret Recipes of an Overcomer, one name shines brightly as a beacon of unwavering support and invaluable guidance – Kadena Tate-Simon.

Kadena, your wisdom, patience, and faith in me have guided this journey, illuminating my path. Your benevolent spirit and ever-present availability gave me the courage to push forward, even in moments of uncertainty. The lessons you shared became the cornerstone that enabled me to build a solid foundation for something even more remarkable than this project–The Literary Lighthouse Alliance, which was inadvertently formed!

You gave me insight into countless possibilities that guided my heart and desires in a land without limits or boundaries. You show me in every interaction that the sky is not the limit! If I wanted to, I am sure you have a resource on how to build a rocket ship, create a strategy, and launch myself to the moon. Even in that, you would have one thousand teachable moments as we soar through the sky.

Although what I am saying may be humorous, it is true. It is your authenticity that has forever left an indelible mark on my heart. You were, and continue to be, an embodiment of the very lessons this book seeks to impart-resilience, faith, and authenticity. You showed me that the power to overcome does not just lie in grand gestures but in every small act of kindness, comforting word, and every moment of selflessness.

From the bottom of my heart, I thank you, Kadena. Thank you for being one of my safe spaces. You are the big sister I used to dream about. I love that your protective side is as active as your nurturing one! You are one of the only people who ever spoke up for me when I was unfairly treated.

I know that it is not something you only did for me. That is just who you are! No one has ever done that for me except for my husband, and I will never forget that act of love.

This book is not just a product of ink and paper – it is a testament to your kind heart, beautiful spirit, and belief in my vision. You are truly one of a kind!

In every sense, you are the secret ingredient in my recipe for success. Thank you for helping me – and, in turn, our readers – embrace the journey from defeat to victory.

FROM THE HEART OF ARLETHA

Dear Readers,

I hope this finds you surrounded by love and filled with a renewed sense of optimism. As the visionary behind, *The Secret Recipes of an Overcomer: How to Transition from Defeat to Victory*, I wanted to take a moment to remind you of something fundamental. You are not alone on this journey. I believe in you with every fiber of my being.

Life can be challenging, my friends. We all face our share of challenges, setbacks, and moments of doubt. But I have learned through my experiences that we are all stronger than we realize. You have the power to overcome any obstacle that stands in your way. Even when it feels like the entire world is against you, remember that I am here, standing by your side and cheering you on. Never, ever give up.

The Secret Recipes of an Overcomer is not just a collection of words on a page; it's a beacon of hope, a guiding light in the darkest times. Within these pages, you will discover the transformative power of resilience, the untapped wellspring of determination that lies within you. You are capable of greatness, my friend, and this will be your roadmap to reclaiming your life, joy, and dreams.

I am honored to be alongside you during this journey. Trust in this process, embrace the challenges that come your way, and never lose sight of your dreams. As you embark on this journey, remember that you are never alone. I am here, cheering you on from the sidelines.

Not only that, but the countless others who will read these words are standing beside you, too. Embrace the challenges, savor the victories, and never forget that the power to overcome resides within you.

With unwavering love and boundless optimism,

Arletha Kent

INTRODUCTION

At first glance, this may seem like any other cookbook, but as you flip through its pages, you'll soon realize that it's much more than that. You're embarking on a journey of transformation – an odyssey narrated by the souls who've navigated the stormy seas of life and emerged stronger, wiser, and braver.

Every author you'll encounter here was once in your shoes, walking through the valley of shadows, burdened with the weight of trials and tribulations. Then, every one of them made it to the other side.

Their victories serve as the main course of our story, offering savory morsels of hope that speak of resilience and courage. Their "secret recipes" are the key ingredients in the feast of life, boldly imparting wisdom that goes far beyond the confines of a traditional recipe book.

As you explore these pages, you will find the authors' steps to overcoming their challenges and a selection of culinary delights that mirror the journey to victory, which is a feast best enjoyed with patience, perseverance, and a dash of bravery.

But this book does more than simply inspire – it empowers. It encourages you to put on the apron of determination, slice through your obstacles, and season your life with the will to prevail. If the heat of the kitchen becomes too much, you will find a list of key resources for additional support, providing a safety net and a reminder that you never have to face these challenges alone.

Every word and recipe is infused with intention, purpose, and hope. With each chapter, you'll find yourself stepping further out of the throes of defeat and closer to the sweetness of victory.

The Secret Recipes of an Overcomer invites you to break bread with us – to be nourished by the shared experiences of others, to partake in their victories, and to savor the delight of turning life's bitterest lemons into the sweetest lemonade. We hope that within these pages, you'll find a beacon of light that helps you navigate your own path. A path that, though peppered with hardship, can lead to a richly satisfying victory.

Are you ready to taste victory? Step into our kitchen. Let's cook up some resilience, stir in some hope, and feast on triumph. After all, like the best meal, victory is best enjoyed after a labor of love.

Welcome to *The Secret Recipes of an Overcomer.*

COLLABORATORS

Uncover divine recipes woven with life's triumphs and challenges, presented within an inspiring guide to faith, resilience, and delectable delights, generously shared by passionate authors. Embark on a journey to reveal both culinary and soulful wisdom.

Arletha S. Kent: Love Glazed BBQ Ribs - 14

Overcoming Invisibility: That's when I realized I was the lighthouse, and my role was to shine my light for others to follow, guiding them through their own stormy seas, ensuring they never felt lost in the darkness.

Rabiah Hogans: Chocolate Upside-Down Cake - 31

Overcoming The Diagnosis: What do you do while you wait in anticipation of taking your last breath?

Travis C. Kent Jr: Tis' So Sweet Potato Pie - 46

Overcoming Codependency: I reflected on my life and realized, to my astonishment, that I'd never been the object of anyone's pursuit.

Diane White: Hot Sautéed Salad - 61

Overcoming Obesity: I knew I had to do something fast, or I would not make it. So, I decided that I was going to live and not die!

Shelyna Tinglin: Jamaican Brown Stew Chicken - 80

Overcoming Past Trauma: I had convinced myself that I was strong enough to handle it on my own and that I didn't need help.

Michael Evans: Stuffed Spicy Chicken Peppers - 96

Overcoming Sex Addiction: To no avail, the taste of women was a drug that drew me back into my indiscretions... but God!

Daletta Lynn: Seafood Medley Bowl - 111

Overcoming The Loss of Innocence: I vividly remember seeing bruises and scars, and it was a constant source of pain and sadness for me.

Charlotte Douglas: Homemade Lasagna - 126

Overcoming a Sheltered Childhood: So, there I was, beautifully sheltered while being a bit naive and socially stagnant.

RESOURCES

Uncover divine recipes woven with life's triumphs and challenges, presented within an inspiring guide to faith, resilience, and delectable delights, generously shared by passionate authors. Embark on a journey to reveal both culinary and soulful wisdom.

Lifelines - Professional Support - 141

These are national lines of support for those seeking specialized help. This can help you overcome any personal challenges, so you can achieve victory.

Shining Stars of Support - 147

Gratitude and recognition for the incredible sponsors whose financial backing ensured a successful collaboration, celebrating our extraordinary new authors.

ARLETHA KENT
Serial Entrepreneur | Author | Mentor

Meet Arletha, a resilient woman of faith who is the heart and soul behind The Literary Lighthouse Alliance. She has triumphed over a lifetime of hurt, disappointments, and stereotypes, finding her purpose in guiding others toward recognition and acceptance. From her early adult years, she shattered barriers, inspiring others. Her journey has led her to be a champion runner for individuals who seek safety, guidance, and empowerment.

Arletha embraces adversity with grace, courage, and tenacity, as evident in her transformative book *inCourage Strengthen from Within*. Her unwavering faith drives her mission: to ensure no one navigates life's stormy seas alone.

LOVE GLAZED BBQ RIBS

"That's when I realized I was the lighthouse, and my role was to shine my light for others to follow, guiding them through their stormy seas and ensuring they never felt lost in the darkness."

INGREDIENTS

- Courage
- Tenacity
- Self-belief
- Faith
- Forgiveness

Overcoming Invisibility

DIRECTIONS

1. Be brave, make bold choices, and face your fears head-on, even if they initially seem impossible.

2. Your determination and unshakeable faith will guide you through any life challenge.

3. Believe in your own strength and worth. Your self-belief will be your shield against all negativities.

4. Keep faith in God and let that faith be your anchor, keeping you grounded even in the most difficult times.

5. Learn to forgive – not to absolve others, but to free yourself from your past chains and create a space for healing and progress.

I am Arletha Kent, the founder and CEO of The Literary Lighthouse Alliance. Like many of yours, my story is one bruised by an ongoing struggle for recognition, despite being filled with achievements.

I've always been a trailblazer, an independent spirit with a natural knack for leadership. But often, my strength was seen as an excuse to neglect me, to bypass the affection and attention I deserved. People around me would compliment my wisdom and determination, but they always felt empty, laced in envy and resentment.

Embodying faith, class, and ambition as an African American woman, I quickly became stereotyped as "holier-than-thou" or "bougie." People also believed that I thought I was perfect. But I refused to be confined by their narrow perceptions. This constant battle to break free from these limitations has shaped my adult life.

High school holds a vivid memory for me. Being one of the fastest girls on the track team, I can still hear the cheers as I ran like it was my last race, my heart pounding in rhythm with my feet hitting the pavement. Yet, despite my victories, and cheers from my friends and their supporters, no one was there specifically for me. No signs, no flowers, no balloons. It felt as if my triumphs were mere expectations being met.

I had my first apartment at 16, while juggling multiple jobs and responsibilities. I was yearning for the nurturing support that other teens took for granted. I would watch their unenthusiastic faces as adults guided them through college applications. I wished I had someone there to walk me through the process and share in my milestones.

At the age of 18, I met the love of my life, Travis. Fast forwarding to age 21, we got married, and together, we opened our hearts and home to foster children and individuals within our community. I mentored many women, but my guidance was often met with envy and resentment. The kindness I extended seemed to sprout thorns, which made me question my approach. I thought about treating people the way they treated me, but I knew that wasn't who I was.

In 2016, during one of the strangest years of my life, I took a bold leap and wrote my first book, *inCourage Strengthen From Within*. Through this process, I found healing, rediscovered my self-worth, and developed an unshakeable faith in God's love for me. This marked the beginning of my true transformation.

However, the path to my destiny was still filled with adversity. I reached a point where I nearly shut down completely. Then, a pivotal vision from God set me on a new course. I am not talking about a mere daydream; this was a divine vision from God Himself.

Imagine this: I was standing beside a vast, dark sea under a pitch-black sky. Not a single star was in sight. It wasn't your typical postcard-worthy scene. It was stormy and dark, like something out of a pirate movie. The sky above matched the intensity of the ocean, a massive black blanket engulfed everything.

The only source of light was this lighthouse, standing tall and strong, shooting out a golden beam across the restless sea. Its light pierced through the darkness like a hot knife through butter. It stood as a sentinel, guarding against the chaos. Four ships sailed toward the lighthouse, their sails filled with the wind, steered by its guiding beam - the light was their compass in the immense darkness.

Out of nowhere, the light flickered. Once, twice, then suddenly, it went out. The entire scene was plunged into darkness. Those four ships became lost and confused shadows. Imagine being out there on the ocean, with no clue where to go, just wandering in the dark.

Then, a moment of intense silence, like the calm before a massive storm. In that stillness, I heard the voice of God. It wrapped around me like a warm blanket, offering insight into my purposes and missions.

"Arletha," He said. "Those ships out there, they seek safety. You cannot turn off your light. You are their guide, their beacon in this chaotic, confusing sea of life. Do not worry about reaching out to them. They will come to you because they need you. All I ask is that you keep shining your light, so they can find their way to safety."

That is when I realized I was the lighthouse, and my role was to shine my light for others to follow, guiding them through their stormy seas and ensuring they never felt lost in the darkness.

At that moment, The Literary Lighthouse Alliance was born. I took the vision I had and embarked on a journey that led me here-leading the Alliance and being a lighthouse for those who are adrift at sea. Creating this community was difficult, but every setback served to strengthen my determination. Here in our community, we do more than just write stories; we validate identities. Our mission is to shatter limiting stereotypes, empower individuals to embrace their authentic selves, and provoke inspiration towards greatness.

If you've ever felt the sting of being overlooked unacknowledged, and unheard know you're not alone. Together, we can rewrite the narrative. Your presence is valued in our community, your choices matter, and you'll find the recognition and support you've always deserved, as we force accountability and work towards a more inclusive and empowering future.

Now, I want to extend a warm invitation to you. Maybe you're feeling like those ships in my vision - lost, unsure, trying to navigate life's challenges. Perhaps you've felt overlooked, yearned for recognition, or grown tired of being boxed into stereotypes. If any of this resonates with you, The Literary Lighthouse Alliance is the perfect place.

Life can be challenging; we all know that. It's like an endless stormy sea. But believe me when I say you don't have to face it alone. In the Alliance, we stand united as a family, a beacon of hope, empowerment, and recognition. We believe in shining our lights brightly, not just being seen but acknowledged and empowered. We understand the struggle of feeling overlooked, desiring for someone to truly see us. We want to ensure no one else feels that way.

So come, be a part of our Alliance. Share your story, struggles, triumphs, and dreams. Let us be your guiding light, offering support and encouragement on your journey. Together, let's overcome invisibility, side by side, each of us shining our unique light.

Remember, your light matters. Your story matters. You matter. Don't hold back. Join us and let's shine together.

Overcoming Invisibility

Inspired by Arletha Kent's Journey

Step 1: Acknowledge Your Journey

Reflect on the challenges and obstacles you've faced in your journey. Write down how these experiences have helped shape who you are today.

Your Reflection:

_____
_____
_____
_____

Step 2: Recognize Your Strengths

List your unique strengths and abilities. Remember, these can be skills, talents, or personal characteristics that make you unique.

Your Unique Strengths:

_____
_____
_____
_____

Step 3: Overcome Stereotypes

Think about any stereotypes or labels you've encountered. Write down how you plan to challenge these perceptions.

Your Strategy:

_____
_____
_____
_____

Step 4: Identify Pivotal Experiences

Consider the significant experiences that have influenced your life. Jot down these moments and how they have shaped you.

Pivotal Experiences:

_____
_____
_____
_____

Step 5: Celebrate Transformation

Reflect on your personal growth over time. Write about a significant transformation you have experienced.

Your Transformation:

_____
_____
_____
_____

Step 6: Apply Your Strengths

Contemplate how you can utilize your strengths to benefit those around you. Write down your thoughts on how you can make a positive impact.

Your Contribution:

_____
_____
_____
_____

Step 7: Seek a Supportive Community

Identify a community that aligns with your values and can provide support. Write down the type of community you wish to be part of.

Ideal Community:

_____

_____

_____

_____

Step 8: Engage Others in Your Journey

Think about how you can involve others in your journey. Write down some ways you can share your experiences and learn from others.

Your Engagement:

_____

_____

_____

_____

Step 9: Commit to Your Personal Growth

Finally, affirm your commitment to personal growth. Write down your mission moving forward.

Your Mission:

_____

_____

_____

_____

Remember, the journey to overcome feelings of invisibility is ongoing. Embrace your unique qualities and let them guide you. You are not alone. Your story, journey, and light matter. Be patient with yourself as you continue on this path.

14-Day Self-Care Checklist for Overlooked Leaders

Use the note pages at the end of this chapter to complete this challenge

DAY 1 AFFIRM YOUR WORTH: WRITE DOWN 5 AFFIRMATIONS THAT REMIND YOU OF YOUR LEADERSHIP QUALITIES.

DAY 2 REFLECT ON OVERCOMING CHALLENGES: JOURNAL ABOUT 3 CHALLENGES YOU'VE OVERCOME THAT MADE YOU A STRONGER LEADER.

DAY 3 GRATITUDE FOR SUPPORT: SEND THANK-YOU NOTES TO 5 PEOPLE WHO HAVE SUPPORTED YOUR LEADERSHIP JOURNEY.

DAY 4 SKILL INVENTORY: LIST 5 SKILLS THAT MAKE YOU A UNIQUE LEADER.

DAY 5 MENTORSHIP: REACH OUT TO A MENTOR OR SOMEONE YOU ADMIRE FOR THEIR LEADERSHIP QUALITIES.

DAY 6 WEEKLY REFLECTION: REFLECT ON THE PAST WEEK'S ACTIVITIES AND JOURNAL YOUR THOUGHTS.

DAY 7 SHARE WISDOM: SHARE A LEADERSHIP TIP OR QUOTE ON SOCIAL MEDIA.

DAY 8 NETWORKING: ATTEND A VIRTUAL OR IN-PERSON NETWORKING EVENT RELATED TO LEADERSHIP.

DAY 9 LEADERSHIP BOOK: START READING A BOOK ON LEADERSHIP AND JOURNAL ANY INSIGHTS.

DAY 10 PUBLIC SPEAKING PRACTICE: RECORD A 5-MINUTE SPEECH ON A LEADERSHIP TOPIC YOU'RE PASSIONATE ABOUT.

DAY 11 SELF-CARE: TAKE A DAY OFF FOR SELF-CARE.

DAY 12 SET BOUNDARIES: SET ONE PERSONAL AND ONE PROFESSIONAL BOUNDARY.

DAY 13 REFLECT: REFLECT ON THE PAST WEEK'S ACTIVITIES. WHAT ARE YOU PROUD OF?

DAY 14 CELEBRATE: CELEBRATE COMPLETING THE 14-DAY CHALLENGE. REFLECT ON HOW FAR YOU'VE COME AND WHAT YOU'VE LEARNED.

Monthly Reflection Journal for Overlooked Leaders

At the end of the month, use the note pages at the end of this chapter to complete this journal to reflect on leadership highs, lows, and growth.

1 Affirmations of the Month: List 3 affirmations that have helped you maintain a positive mindset as a leader.

_____

_____

2 Leadership Highlights: Write down 3 significant leadership moments or achievements from this month.

_____

_____

3 Challenges Overcome: Describe 2 challenges you faced and how you overcame them.

_____

_____

4 Gratitude: Identify two individuals who have been your pillars of support this month and explain how.

_____

_____

5 Skills and Growth: Identify 1 skill you've improved upon and how it has made you a better leader.

_____

_____

6 Final Reflections: Write a few sentences summarizing your leadership journey this month.

_____

_____

LOVE GLAZED BBQ RIBS

Love Glazed BBQ Ribs are a heart-stealing masterpiece, combining tender marinated ribs with a smoky rub, nestled among onions and bell peppers, and crowned with a caramelized BBQ sauce, delivering a love-filled symphony with every bite.

Recipe from the heart of
Arletha Kent

DIRECTIONS

1. **Prep**: Peel off the membrane from the ribs back, for tenderness, and marinate them in Olive Garden Italian Dressing for a 30-minute fridge.

2. **Preheat**: Set your oven at 350 °F. or increase heat to 400 °F for a shorter baking time (1.5-2hrs).

3. **Season**: Coat ribs with mustard. Mix brown sugar, smoked paprika, pepper, salt, chili, garlic and onion powders, cayenne, and oregano to form a dry rub. Apply rub over ribs.

4. **Prepare for Baking**: Lay each rack on a double-layered aluminum foil bed with sliced onions and bell peppers underneath, and wrap tightly.

5. **Bake**: Position foil-wrapped ribs on a baking sheet and bake for 2.5-3 hours until tender.

6. **Finishing and Serving**: After baking, apply BBQ sauce and broil/grill for 5 mins/side. Rest, slice, and serve with onions, bell peppers, and extra sauce.

SERVINGS	PREP	COOKING
4-6	60 min	3 hrs (approx.)

INGREDIENTS

- 2 St. Louis rib racks
- 1/4 cup each of brown sugar and smoked paprika
- 1 tbsp. each of black pepper, salt, chili powder, garlic powder, onion powder, and dried oregano
- 1 tsp. cayenne pepper
- 2 cups each of mustard (Yellow/Dijon) and Italian dressing (e.g., Olive Garden)
- BBQ sauce of choice
- 2 sliced onions
- 2 sliced bell peppers (any color)

Don't allow what you feel to override what you know.

Arletha Kent

RABIAH HOGANS

Entrepreneur | Author

Meet Rabiah, a survivor of a Traumatic Brain Injury who has defied the odds. Through sheer determination and unwavering faith, Rabiah survived cerebellar degeneration and thrived beyond all expectations.

She is the CEO of Variable Professional Solutions, a notary and fingerprinting business. Being a graduate of Grand Canyon University, her academic background in Accounting (BSA) and teaching both General & Special Education (MAT), along with her expertise in medical coding, makes her a testament to the Power of God!

CHOCOLATE UPSIDE-DOWN CAKE

"What do you do while you wait in anticipation of taking your last breath?"

INGREDIENTS

- Transparency
- Determination
- Courage
- Faithfulness
- Resilience

Overcoming The Diagnosis

DIRECTIONS

1. Acknowledge and accept areas of improvement in your life.

2. Seek resources to make the necessary changes. (Church, therapy, support groups, etc.)

3. Be open to guidance, constructive criticism, and correction.

4. Diligently work on making the necessary changes.

5. Don't allow anything or anyone to deter you from your God-given purpose.

In April 2003, my life changed forever after a night of partying and arriving home at 3 a.m., waking up at 6 a.m. to a typical day of classes starting at 7:30 a.m. After my classes, I had to work. Once my shift was over and I made it through rush hour traffic, I was extremely sleepy, so I decided to go and take a nap at my mother's house.

I woke up feeling disoriented and nauseous, and my eyes were involuntarily moving side-to-side and up and down in a circular motion. I attempted to stand but collapsed repeatedly, unable to coordinate my movements.

This morning my mother was at work, so I had to crawl to the phone to call for help. I called her job, and she sent an ambulance to rush me to the hospital. After an MRI and a spinal tap, the doctors delivered the devastating news that I had a rare traumatic brain injury called cerebellar degeneration, and I only had six months to live.

My body would slowly shut down until I was in a vegetative state. Only 3% of the American population had this diagnosis and little to no research on a cure or treatment.

I was devastated. Reflecting on my life, I realized how reckless and self-destructive I had been, often forgetting that life is truly short-lived. In James 4:14 NKJV, the Word of God says, "Whereas you do not know what will happen tomorrow. For what is your life? It is even a vapor that appears for a little time and then vanishes away."

During that time, I thought I was living my best life. I never thought in a million years that at 28, my behavior would be the impression I would make in the world.

I blamed God and believed He was angry with me. I contemplated suicide but was too weak to carry it out. I felt helpless, angry, and mad at Him that my life was ending this way. I felt like the punishment did not fit the crime. I did not believe I had done so wrong that I deserved to die this way.

There was nothing else the doctors could do for me, so they sent me home to be comfortable and prepare for my death. What do you do while you wait in anticipation of taking your last breath? Prayer was not an option because I thought God was mad at me.

I was so lost and confused with my spirituality. Being raised in the Islamic faith, we physically got on our knees to perform salat or prayer. But because of my physical disposition, this was not an option for me. I desperately wanted to reconcile with God, but I did not know how.

That all changed when one of my Christian friends wanted to visit. However, he had health challenges that would not allow him to travel at the time, so he reached out to a local Church of God to request prayer for me. I was so shocked that the Pastor and his wife personally came to my house. They embraced and supported me. They didn't judge me for being a Muslim. It was as if they didn't care. Their focus was sharing the love of Christ.

They would come to my home every week to pray and have bible study. It was then I learned about the miracles of Christ. I learned how to pray to God and was taught there are no limitations when speaking and connecting with Him.

I could lay in my bed, cry to God, and believe He was with me. I learned to understand the Word of God by listening to audio bible Scriptures, which helped since I was going blind.

I repented, dedicated my life to the Lord, and found peace with the fact that God wasn't punishing me. I accepted the reality that He loved me! I learned that the doctors were doing their job, but God had the final say!

"But He was wounded for our transgressions,
He was bruised for our iniquities;
The chastisement for our peace was upon Him,
And by His stripes, we are healed."
Isaiah 53:5 NKJV

Three months into my six-month death sentence, I fell asleep watching TV, but something woke me up. When I opened my eyes, with blurred vision, I saw a man sitting on the end of my bed, and he told me everything would be all right. I fell back to sleep.

When I woke up, that tightness in my chest and stomach caused by the guilt and shame that God was upset with me had lifted. I truly felt free and believed that I was going to be OK. I started to experience hope and seek God for my purpose.

Fast forward to the sixth month, October of 2003, I had a revelation...I WAS STILL ALIVE! I received a miracle which meant I still had choices, even if they were limited. I decided to apply to college, even though I could barely see, walk, speak, or write.

I applied online, using the brief moments when my eyesight was still enough to navigate the website. To my surprise, I was accepted. I called my social worker, who arranged accommodations like a note-taker, transportation, and tutoring services.

On my first day of class, a man in a suit picked me up and drove me to school. A woman met me at the door and showed me around. A note-taker was waiting for me in the classroom. I was amazed at the support I received.

Over time, I got the hang of attending school and earned my associate degree. I earned my master's degree and, 20 years later, have continued to live a fulfilling life. By God's grace, I am a college graduate, business owner, and author.

It amazes me how the power of God transformed my life. I went from feeling powerless to realizing that I still had so much life to live.

By my deciding to follow God's lead through a mustard seed size faith, He was able to fulfill His Glory in my life. I am still in recovery through physical therapy and other recommended treatments. I am exceeding the doctors' expectations. They are continuously surprised at my progress.

I want everyone to know that even in the darkest times, God never brings you to a place that His grace can't get you through.

Overcoming The Diagnosis

Inspired by Rabiah Hogan's Journey

Step 1: Acknowledge Your Diagnosis

Rabiah's story began with a life-changing diagnosis. Take a moment to reflect on your own diagnosis. Write it down and describe how it has affected you physically and emotionally.

Your Diagnosis:

_____

Your Experience:

_____

_____

_____

_____

Step 2: Reflect on Your Pre-Diagnosis Life

Rabiah reflected on her life before the diagnosis, where she lived with reckless behavior. Contemplate your life before your diagnosis. What are the habits or lifestyle choices you regret or cherish? Jot them down.

Your Pre-Diagnosis Life:

_____

_____

_____

_____

Step 3: Emotional Response

Rabiah experienced a range of emotions, including fear, anger, and helplessness. Recognize your emotional response to the diagnosis. It is important to allow yourself to feel these emotions without judgment.

Your Emotions:

_____

_____

_____

_____

Step 4: Seek Spiritual Solace

In her despair, Rabiah found comfort and guidance in her faith. Consider seeking solace through your own spiritual practices. This can take many forms, such as prayer, meditation, or spending time in nature.

Your Spiritual Solace:

_____

_____

_____

_____

Step 5: Connect with Others

The support from Rabiah's Christian friends and their pastor made a significant impact on her journey. Think about who in your life you can reach out to for emotional and spiritual support.

Your Support Network:

_____

_____

_____

_____

Step 6: Reassess Your Beliefs

Rabiah realized that her suffering was not a divine punishment, but a challenge she had to face. Reflect on your beliefs about your diagnosis. Do you see it as a punishment, a test, or something else entirely?

Your Beliefs:

_____

_____

_____

Step 7: Seek Hope and Purpose

Rabiah experienced hope and started seeking her purpose after a divine vision. Consider what gives you hope and what purpose you can find in your situation.

Your Hope:

_____
_____
_____
_____

Your Purpose:

_____
_____
_____
_____

Step 8: Embrace Your New Normal

Despite her physical limitations, Rabiah decided to apply to college, demonstrating a courageous embrace of her new normal. Think about ways you can embrace your own "new normal" and write down actionable steps.

Your New Normal:

_____
_____
_____
_____

Step 9: Cherish Your Achievements

Rabiah celebrated her achievements, such as earning her degrees and running her business. Reflect on your own achievements, however big or small, since your diagnosis.

Your Achievements:

_____
_____
_____

Step 10: Advocate for Your Progress

Rabiah continues her recovery journey and exceeds doctors' expectations. Write down your recovery plan and how you can advocate for your progress.

Your Recovery Plan:

_____

_____

_____

_____

Recognizing your diagnosis and understanding its impact is essential. However, it's equally crucial to draw from the power of your inner resilience, lean on your support network, and draw strength from the hope and purpose that stem from your journey. Keep pushing forward, believing in yourself, and seeking the positive in every situation.

BRAINSTORMING

THROUGH THE DYNAMIC PROCESS OF ACTION BRAINSTORMING, YOU CAN PINPOINT THE ELEMENTS THAT ARE EITHER PROPELLING YOU TOWARDS OR HINDERING YOU FROM ATTAINING YOUR OBJECTIVES.

MY GOAL:

STOP DOING

DO LESS OF

KEEP DOING

DO MORE OF

START DOING

CHOCOLATE UPSIDE-DOWN CAKE

Savor the irresistible combination of rich chocolate, crunchy pecans, and succulent strawberries in this delightful Chocolate Upside Down Cake with a caramel twist.

Recipe from the heart of
Arletha Kent

DIRECTIONS

1. **Prep**:
   - Preheat oven to 350 °F.
   - Grease a 9-inch round cake pan.

2. **Make Caramel Layer**:
   - Mix melted butter and light brown sugar.
   - Spread mixture in cake pan.
   - Drizzle half of caramel sauce.
   - Add strawberries and pecans.

3. **Make Cake Batter**
   - Whisk flour, cocoa powder, baking powder, and salt.
   - In another bowl, mix granulated sugar, egg, and vanilla.
   - Combine wet and dry ingredients, adding milk gradually.
   - Fold in chocolate chips.

4. **Bake the Cake**:
   - Pour batter over caramel layer in pan.
   - Bake for 40-45 minutes.
   - Cool in pan for 15 minutes.

5. **Invert and Serve**:
   - Invert cake onto a plate.
   - Drizzle remaining caramel sauce.
   - Cool completely before slicing and serving.

SERVINGS	PREP	COOKING
8-10	20 min	40 min

INGREDIENTS

- 1 stick unsalted butter, melted
- 1 cup light brown sugar
- 1 cup flour
- 1/2 cup cocoa powder
- 1 1/2 tsps. baking powder
- 1/2 tsp. salt
- 1/2 cup granulated sugar
- 1 large egg
- 1 tsp. vanilla extract
- 1/2 cup milk
- 1 cup chocolate chips
- 1 1/2 cups sliced strawberries
- 1/2 cup chopped pecans
- 1/2 cup caramel sauce
(store bought or make from scratch)

> Even in the darkest of times, God never brings you to a place that His grace can't bring you through.
>
> *Rabiah Hogans*

TRAVIS C. KENT JR.

Entrepreneur | Author | Singer

Meet Travis, an Entrepreneur, Author, and anointed Singer, who shares his compelling journey of self-discovery and personal growth. His story delves into his struggles with prioritizing others over himself, ultimately leading him to realize his self-worth, embrace the power of saying "no," and prioritize his well-being.

At 37, a life-changing revelation transformed Travis from a self-sacrificing individual into a resilient and empowered one. Travis' story inspires readers to challenge their beliefs, rediscover their self-worth, and embrace the healing power of forgiveness.

TIS SO SWEET POTATO PIE

"I reflected on my life and realized, to my astonishment, that I'd never been the object of anyone's pursuit."

INGREDIENTS

- Self-Care
- Set Boundaries
- Assessment
- Self-Awareness
- Forgiveness

Overcoming Codependency

DIRECTIONS

1. Prioritize your needs by recognizing that self-care is essential for healthy relationships.

2. Practice saying 'no' when necessary and without justifying your decision.

3. Acknowledge and address any relationships that are hindering your progress by letting them go.

4. Be aware of your motivations for wanting to be needed by others.

5. Practice forgiveness to safeguard your heart from bitterness and embrace all God has in store for you.

Throughout my life, I've consistently prioritized the happiness and satisfaction of others, often neglecting my own needs. As a child, I frequently prioritized my sisters, sacrificing my necessities to ensure theirs were met. Raised in a loving two-parent home, we faced our share of financial hardships.

During those times, I chose to do without new clothes so my sisters could have them, subsequently facing mockery at school. I distinctly recall wearing shoes so worn out that the toes curled up. To mask my embarrassment and pain, I embraced the role of a class clown, jokingly claiming to be an elf. This coping mechanism would shape my response to difficult situations well into adulthood.

During high school, depression developed, leading me to believe I was unattractive and undeserving of a girlfriend. This negative self-image was reinforced by certain family members who, under the devil's influence, convinced me they were superior in looks and worth. This led me to always consider myself last in every scenario.

When I found a girl, I was fond of, I inflicted emotional pain upon myself. I put myself in situations where I would witness her kissing another guy at his doorstep while remembering that I was just a friend, undeserving of such intimate experiences.

In time, I found authentic love in my wife of 23 years. Still, the enduring impact of my past thinking continued to shadow even our marriage. Overjoyed to be wanted, I played the part of who she believed I was, who I pretended to be, and who I aspired to be, oblivious that this disguise could only last for so long before the authentic me would surface.

My primary objective was her happiness. I even addressed what she had missed in her childhood by agreeing to provide a safe haven for children who didn't ask to be with us but whom we felt needed us for their security and welfare. This continued the cycle of prioritizing others' needs over my own.

Subsequently, I answered the Lord's call to shepherd His flock. We passionately began welcoming people into our home, adopting families, donating furniture and cars, covering rent, mortgages, and utilities, and sacrificing our privacy to ensure others never felt isolated. Our actions often lacked wisdom, hurting us by the absence of gratitude. Each instance reinforced the falsehood that my happiness didn't matter to anyone.

Over time, resentment began to take root in my heart, leading me to grow cold toward the individuals I was called to lead. How could I effectively shepherd a flock that I was starting to detest? How could I offer the Lord rewards for His suffering when these rewards were the very souls I was beginning to resent?

I found myself at a crossroads, confronted by a stark reality: if I couldn't live in service to Him, why should I be granted life? My desire to please Him never waned despite feeling shackled by something elusive. During this period of pastoring, I was blessed with a revelatory teaching anointing.

As I delved into the Word of God daily, it began to mold my heart, preparing me to receive a profound revelation that would otherwise have eluded me.

One evening, my wife posed a question that would shake my core, "Travis, you've always been the pursuer in your relationships, but has anyone ever pursued you?" I reflected on my life and realized that I'd never been the object of anyone's pursuit.

Every relationship I had was a result of my own relentless efforts. It would wither away if I didn't initiate contact or try to maintain the bond. This revelation was a bitter pill to swallow, but it marked a crucial milestone on my journey to recovery.

Reflecting on my past, I realize I relied on various coping mechanisms to navigate difficult times. However, thanks to the guidance of the Holy Spirit, I am now equipped to maintain my freedom from the shackles that held me captive. By embracing principles from the Word of God, I can implement changes that lead to triumph over life's challenges. Allow me to share with you five of these transformative principles.

First, I had to recondition my mind with the truth that I am valuable. I had been putting everyone else's needs before my own, but I started to meditate on Isaiah 43:1 NKJV, which states, *"But now, thus says the Lord, He who created you, O Jacob (Travis), He who formed you, O Israel (Travis): Fear not, for I have redeemed you, I have called you by your name; You are mine."*

This realization brought a new perspective to my life; I no longer needed to sacrifice my needs for others because I knew I was valued by God and had unlimited access to fellowship with Him. Recognizing my worth fortified my relationships as I began appreciating and loving myself. As a result, all my relationships benefited from what I had to offer.

The second practice was learning the importance of saying "no" when necessary. I realized that "no" is a complete sentence, requiring no additional supporting evidence. It was liberating to realize that I didn't need to justify my decisions or lie to avoid hurting someone's feelings.

Jesus emphasized this principle's importance in Matthew 5:37 NKJV when He said, *"But let your 'Yes' be 'Yes' and your 'No,' 'No.' For whatever is more than these is from the evil one."* It is not my responsibility to manage someone else's emotions if they are unhappy with my decision to say no. I have discovered a healthier way of living by putting this principle into practice.

The third practice was acknowledging that only some in your inner circle are meant to join you on your journey. Those closest to you, including family, may not join you in the next level of life. This was a difficult lesson I had to learn. In Luke 14:26 AMP, Jesus says, *"If anyone comes to me and does not hate father and mother, wife and children, brothers and sisters, yes, and his own life, he cannot follow me."*

I realized "hate" meant the cost or value of following Him. When we truly follow Him, it may come at the expense of some of our closest relationships. Refusing to let go of these relationships can hinder our progress. Ultimately, the question comes down to how much we value answering the call to follow Him.

The fourth practice was discerning the difference between being needed by someone and needing to be needed by someone. A particular chapter in my wife's book *inCourage Strengthened From Within* prompted me to re-evaluate my perspective. Upon reflection, I realized that most of the people I believed needed me in their lives did not.

Instead, it was me who needed them to need me. I felt hurt and disappointed when they displayed that they didn't need me. It wasn't their fault because my self-imposed wound of desiring to be needed caused the pain.

The fifth practice I adopted was to safeguard my heart. People can inflict unimaginable pain on us, causing us tremendous heartache. Unfortunately, we cannot experience the full beauty that God has in store for us without interacting with others because He blesses us through them.

I had to learn to protect my heart after struggling with bitterness. It's a subtle spirit that creeps in when we've been hurt multiple times. The most effective way I learned to guard my heart was through the power of forgiveness.

Paul wrote in Ephesians 4:32 KJV, *"Be kind to one another, tenderhearted, forgiving one another, as God in Christ forgave you."* Learning to forgive others brought a newfound sense of freedom into my life. Practicing forgiveness positioned me to safeguard and protect my heart while simultaneously enjoying the journey of this abundant life that Jesus came to give us.

Overcoming Codependency

Inspired by Travis C. Kent Jr.'s Journey

In light of Travis story, here are five practical exercises to help you combat codependency.

Exercise 1: Embrace Your Self-Worth
Reflect on the ways you've been sacrificing your needs for others. Write them down:

_____
_____
_____
_____

Now, meditate on Isaiah 43:1 NKJV:

"But now, thus says the Lord, He who created you, O Jacob (Your Name), He who formed you, O Israel (Your Name): 'Fear not, for I have redeemed you, I have called you by your name; You are mine."

Write down what this scripture means for your personal worth. How will embracing this perspective influence your relationships and interactions with others?

_____
_____
_____
_____

Exercise 2: Mastering the Art of Saying "No"
Identify scenarios in your life where you struggle to say "no." Describe why it's challenging for you.

_____
_____
_____
_____

Now, consider Matthew 5:37 NKJV:

"But let your 'Yes' be 'Yes' and your 'No,' 'No.' For whatever is more than these is from the evil one."

Write down how applying this principle can alter these situations and what changes you can implement to assert your boundaries better.

_____
_____
_____
_____

Exercise 3: Letting Go When Necessary

Think about the relationships in your life that may not serve you as you progress. Contemplate Luke 14:26 NKJV.

"If anyone comes to Me and does not hate his father and mother, wife and children, brothers and sisters, yes, and his own life also, he cannot be My disciple."

Describe how this verse relates to these relationships. Write down the steps you are willing to take to make room for your personal growth.

_____
_____
_____
_____

Exercise 4: Discern Between Being Needed and Needing to Be Needed

Reflect on the relationships where you felt a strong need to be needed. Considering your reflection, write down how these relationships would transform if you detached your self-worth from being needed.

_____
_____
_____
_____

Exercise 5: Safeguarding Your Heart Through Forgiveness

Identify instances where you've been deeply hurt and struggled with resentment. Use Ephesians 4:32 NKJV as a guide.

"And be kind to one another, tenderhearted, forgiving one another, even as God in Christ forgave you."

Describe how applying the principle of forgiveness can influence these situations and your overall well-being.

_____

_____

_____

_____

As you complete these exercises, remember that overcoming codependency is a gradual process that requires time, patience, and perseverance. It's about continually prioritizing your needs and setting boundaries while maintaining healthy and balanced relationships.

Travis' journey is a powerful testament that change is possible, and his transformation can inspire you to create your own recovery story.

CHECKLIST

Self-care Affirmations

1	I am worthy of love and respect.
2	I am in control of my own happiness.
3	I am capable of great things.
4	I am allowed to make mistakes and learn from them.
5	I am allowed to take care of myself.
6	I am allowed to put myself first.
7	I am allowed to take breaks when I need them.
8	I am allowed to say no.
9	I am allowed to be assertive.
10	I am allowed to take care of my own needs.

30 Self-Care Challenges

○ Write and recite 5 positive affirmations	○ Write a letter to your future self	○ Go for a walk in nature	○ Indulge in your favorite treat	○ Go to bed earlier
○ Listen to favorite song	○ Eat vegetarian meals	○ Take a nice bubble bath	○ Cook your favorite meal	○ Strech your body before bed
○ Go on a solo date	○ Journal for 15 minutes	○ Give yourself a facial	○ Practice Self gratitude	○ Try a DIY Project
○ Read a book	○ Create a piece of Art	○ Enjoy laughter Therapy	○ Watch your favorite movie	○ Mindful breathing practice
○ Give yourself a break	○ Watch the sunrise	○ Create your ideal future	○ Watch the sunset	○ Start a new hobby
○ Aromatherapy	○ Music Therapy	○ Celebrate You	○ Digital Detox	○ Dance Break

TIS' SO SWEET POTATO PIE

Indulge in the heavenly delight of Tis' So Sweet Potato Pie, where the comforting embrace of sweet potatoes, warm spices, and a flaky crust creates a harmonious symphony of flavors.

SERVINGS	PREP	COOKING
8	30 min	55-60 min

INGREDIENTS

- 1 1/2 cups all-purpose flour, 1/2 tsp salt, 1/2 cup chilled unsalted butter
- 4-5 tbsps. ice water, 2 cups mashed sweet potatoes
- 1 cup granulated sugar, 1 cup packed brown sugar
- 1/2 cup whole milk, 1/4 cup melted unsalted butter
- 3 large beaten eggs, 1 tsp. vanilla extract
- 1 1/2 tsps. combined ground cinnamon and nutmeg, 1/4 tsp. salt
- 1 cup heavy cream, 2 tbsps. powdered sugar

Recipe from the heart of
Arletha Kent

DIRECTIONS

1. **Prep**: Combine flour, salt, and chilled butter. Add ice water and shape dough into a disk. Chill for 30 minutes.

2. **Preheat**: Set oven to 350°F.

3. **Prepare Filling**: Mix mashed sweet potatoes, sugars, milk, melted butter, eggs, vanilla, cinnamon, nutmeg.

4. **Roll & Place**: Roll chilled dough, fit into a 9-inch pie dish, trim and crimp edges.

5. **Bake**: Bake pie for 55-60 minutes until set. Cool to room temperature.

6. **Serve**: Delight in Southern Sweet Potato Pie's flavors with loved ones.

> Renewing our minds, embracing boundaries, and forgiving others transforms brokenness into wholeness.
>
> *Travis C. Kent Jr.*

DIANE WHITE
Evangelist | Author

Meet Diane, an evangelist, and mother of four who conquered obesity and other health challenges with unwavering faith and determination. Serving under Bishop Terance E. Coleman at Greater Pentecostal Church of God, Diane has held numerous roles, including Director of the Greeters Ministry and Intercessor Ministry.

A licensed evangelist under Higher Ground International Ministries and a Bethesda Temple Bible Institute graduate, her passion for soul-winning has been proven by results from over 90 baptisms through her uniquely designed outreach programs facilitated at local laundromats and the St. Louis Job Corps Center. Dive into her inspiring journey to discover the power of unwavering faith and perseverance.

HOT SAUTEÉD SALAD

"I knew I had to do something fast, or I would not make it. So, I decided that I was going to live and not die!"

INGREDIENTS

- Steadfastness
- A Regimen
- Will Power
- Patience
- Tenacity

Overcoming Obesity

DIRECTIONS

1. Embrace steadfastness by committing to your weight loss journey with unwavering dedication.

2. Develop a personalized regimen that includes a balanced diet and regular exercise.

3. Harness your willpower to resist unhealthy temptations and stay on track.

4. Practice patience, understanding that weight loss is a gradual process requiring time and perseverance.

5. Display tenacity by pushing through challenging moments and setbacks to reach your goals.

There I was, 65 years old and weighing a massive 425 pounds. My body was a mess, dealing with high blood pressure, diabetes, and degenerative disc disease. I was taking three different meds for blood pressure, popping 100 milligrams of metformin twice a day, and even 10 milligrams of oxycodone, six times a day, couldn't keep the pain in check.

Osteoarthritis joined the party, too, forcing me to take even more pills. Here is where 7.25 milligrams of Meloxicam, three times a day, was added to my pain cocktail. My right hip was in such a bad shape that I needed a hip replacement. Still, there were so many requirements to meet before I could even consider qualifying for one, including having a BMI lower than 40. In the meantime, I tried to find some relief with hip and knee injections.

I am a recovering drug addict. I used crack cocaine for over 25 years. This made taking those heavy narcotics a huge risk for me. But, by the grace of God, I was shielded from relapse.

All of this led to me needing a walker. And if that was not enough, I discovered I might have spinal stenosis caused by osteoarthritis resulting in yet another pain injection in my back. I also had to see a heart doctor, who had me wear a heart monitor for a week. They found that I needed a CPAP machine to sleep.

I could not believe it. At the age of 66, I took over ten different types of pills, received three injections, used a walker, and struggled to sleep with a CPAP machine. I knew I had to do something fast or I would not make it. I decided that I was going to live and not die!

I heard that weight loss surgery was available for Medicaid recipients, and I had Medicaid at the time. I excitedly went to the classes, eager to learn about the program. I was all in, attending classes and doing everything they asked until they hit me with the six-week liquid diet requirement. That is when I hit the brakes!

Between family losses and the terrifying idea of going six weeks without a single bite of solid food, my motivation disappeared faster than a pizza at a sleepover. So, I gracefully bowed out of the program.

Fast forward a few months, and there I was, still munching on whatever I wanted, not giving my weight a second thought - except for the occasional guilt trip. But the pain, oh, the pain! It was everywhere, like an uninvited guest at a party.

My pain management doctor kept preaching the gospel of the keto diet, but I just was not feeling it. Yet, I knew something had to give. My life had become a sad cycle of doctor visits, eating, pain pills, sleep, and repeat. I was like a broken record, constantly battling pain and getting injections in my hip, back, and knees.

Finally, I cried to the Lord, "I need to lose this weight, but I don't know how!" He answered my prayer.

I was led to give the keto diet a shot-my version of it, anyway. I started saying goodbye to fast food, junk food, and those tempting zoo zoos and wham whams, like cupcakes, sodas, and chips. And, oh boy, do not even get me started on the mouthwatering dinners I used to whip up, complete with peach cobblers, mac and cheese, cheesecakes, and my all-time favorite, Dutch apple pie from Sam's!

But I had to cut all that goodness out, even the scrumptious pecan pies. And guess what? After a month of ditching my bad habits, I saw a difference! Hallelujah! The weight began falling off, and I was not even exercising - just cutting back on the goodies. And lo and behold, I lost 10 to 15 pounds a month!

I shared my progress with my goddaughter Arletha, and she was so proud of me!

"Ma, take it up a notch," she said.

"What do you mean, take it up a notch?" I asked.

"Walk," she replied.

"Girl, you must be joking! Me, walking with a walker? No way!"

She urged, "Ma, just take your time. Walk one house down the street and come back. Just do your best and each time set a new goal...one house, two houses, three houses all the way to the end of the block and you'll see the difference it'll make! You can do it!"

I was still skeptical, especially with my trusty walker. But that night, the Lord showed me in a dream walking down my street. I yelled out, "Oh my God, on the walker!"

The Lord told me to walk down three houses and back three times a week. I sat up in bed, wide-eyed, and said, "The Father, the Son, and the Holy Spirit!" I could not wait for my aide to arrive the next day. So, I began walking three houses down and back three times a week-Mondays, Wednesdays, and Fridays.

I would get my aide to film me walking down just one house and back, that's all I was ready for the world to see. Three houses felt like too much, as I'd get tired and need to rest in between. But even during my struggle, people driving by would honk their horns in support, cheering me on.

The feedback from the videos I posted on Facebook was incredible. As I kept up with the walking, the weight really started dropping off. Instead of losing 10 to 15 pounds a month, it was now 20 to 25! I tried everything, but I had yet to get this far. Even when the weather turned, my loving family bought me a treadmill to keep me going.

My doctor was amazed! Little did he know, I was still sneaking sugar, just not as much. On the keto diet, you are supposed to cut out sugar altogether, so I replaced my usual candy with fruit. Now I had reached a point where I did not crave much of anything and did not want to cook!

I'm so grateful to the Lord for giving me a plan! I thank Him for giving me the mindset to change and rethink my food choices. Yes, I needed a made-up mind and the will to live because I was eating myself to death! It's called gluttonous eating, which is a thing of my past.

Within 19 months, I have lost over 200 pounds, am off Metformin and Oxycodone, and only have two injections per year. I also don't use a CPAP machine, only take one blood pressure pill, and Meloxicam twice a month.

Hallelujah! I feel so much better. I still have a few goals to hit but I am well on my way! I will soon be eligible for body contouring surgery-with insurance covering the bill, praise the Lord!

If you are reading this story and struggling with weight loss or any other struggle, remember that a determined mind and willpower are the keys to success. You, too, can live and declare the works of the Lord and conquer obesity.

Overcoming Obesity

Inspired by Diane White's Journey

Exercise 1: Recognizing the Problem

Write down the health issues you're currently dealing with as a result of your obesity.

_____

_____

_____

_____

List the medication you are currently taking, and what each one is for.

_____

_____

_____

_____

Take note of any physical limitations caused by your weight.

_____

_____

_____

_____

Reflect on your emotional state. How does your weight affect your mood, self-esteem, and relationships?

_____

_____

_____

_____

Take note of any addiction issues you might be dealing with in addition to your weight problem.

_____

_____

_____

_____

Exercise 2: Getting Ready for Change

Write down why you want to lose weight. Be as specific as possible.

_____

_____

_____

_____

List any unsuccessful attempts you've made to lose weight in the past. What were the roadblocks?

_____

_____

_____

_____

Identify what's different this time. What is motivating you now?

_____

_____

_____

_____

Reflect on your diet. What unhealthy foods do you consume regularly?

_____

_____

_____

_____

Note any specific meals or snacks that you know are high in sugar, unhealthy fats or high in calories that you enjoy.

_____

_____

_____

_____

Exercise 3: Setting Goals and Making a Plan
Make a list of unhealthy foods you are willing to give up, or cut back on, starting today.

_____

_____

_____

_____

Set a realistic weight loss goal for the first month.

_____

_____

_____

_____

Consider adding a simple form of exercise to your routine. This could be walking, like Diane did, or something else you would enjoy. Set a goal for how often you will do this exercise.

_____

_____

_____

_____

Reflect on any support you might have in your life. Is there someone who could be your cheerleader, like Diane's goddaughter was for her?

_____

_____

_____

_____

Exercise 4: Celebrating Progress and Staying Motivated

A. **Instructions:** At the end of this chapter there are trackers and note pages to assist you in completing this exercise.

- Keep track of your weight loss. Write down how much you are losing each month.
- Celebrate your successes, no matter how small they might seem.

Write down every success, so you can look back at them when you need motivation.

B. **Instructions:** Assess Each Month

1. Reflect on your journey. Have your health, mood, and self-esteem improved? If so, how?
2. Are you facing any new challenges? How can you overcome them?

Remember, overcoming obesity is not about quick fixes or temporary diets. It is about creating sustainable changes in your lifestyle. With determination and the right mindset, you can conquer obesity, just like Diane did.

Measurement Tracker

Start Date: ___ / ___ / ___

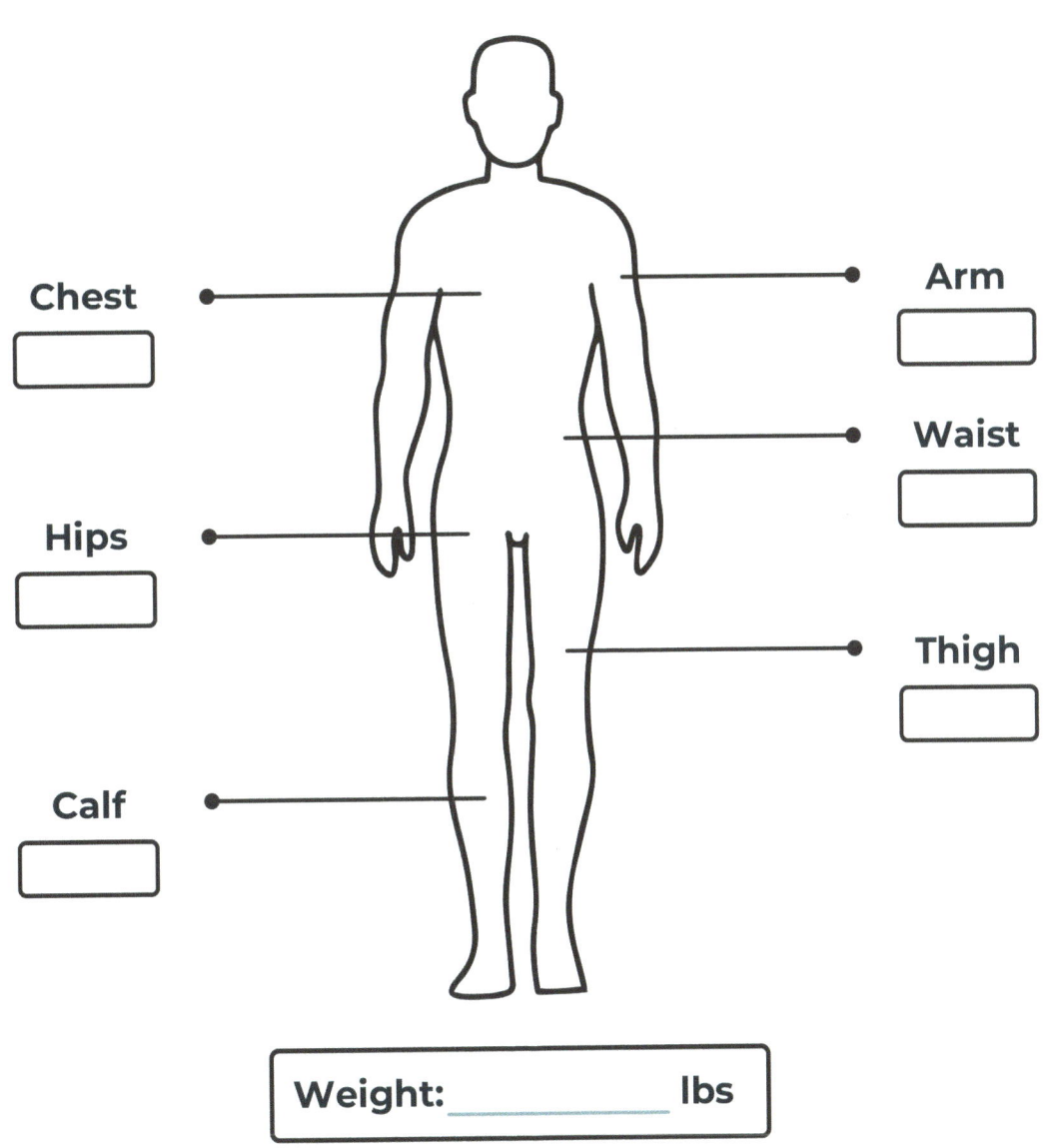

Chest

Arm

Hips

Waist

Calf

Thigh

Weight: _____ lbs

My Weight Loss Journey

	Starting Weight	Ending Weight	+/- Pounds
Week 1			
Week 2			
Week 3			
Week 4			
Week 5			
Week 6			
Week 7			
Week 8			
Week 9			
Week 10			

Measurement Tracker

End Date: ___ / ___ / ___

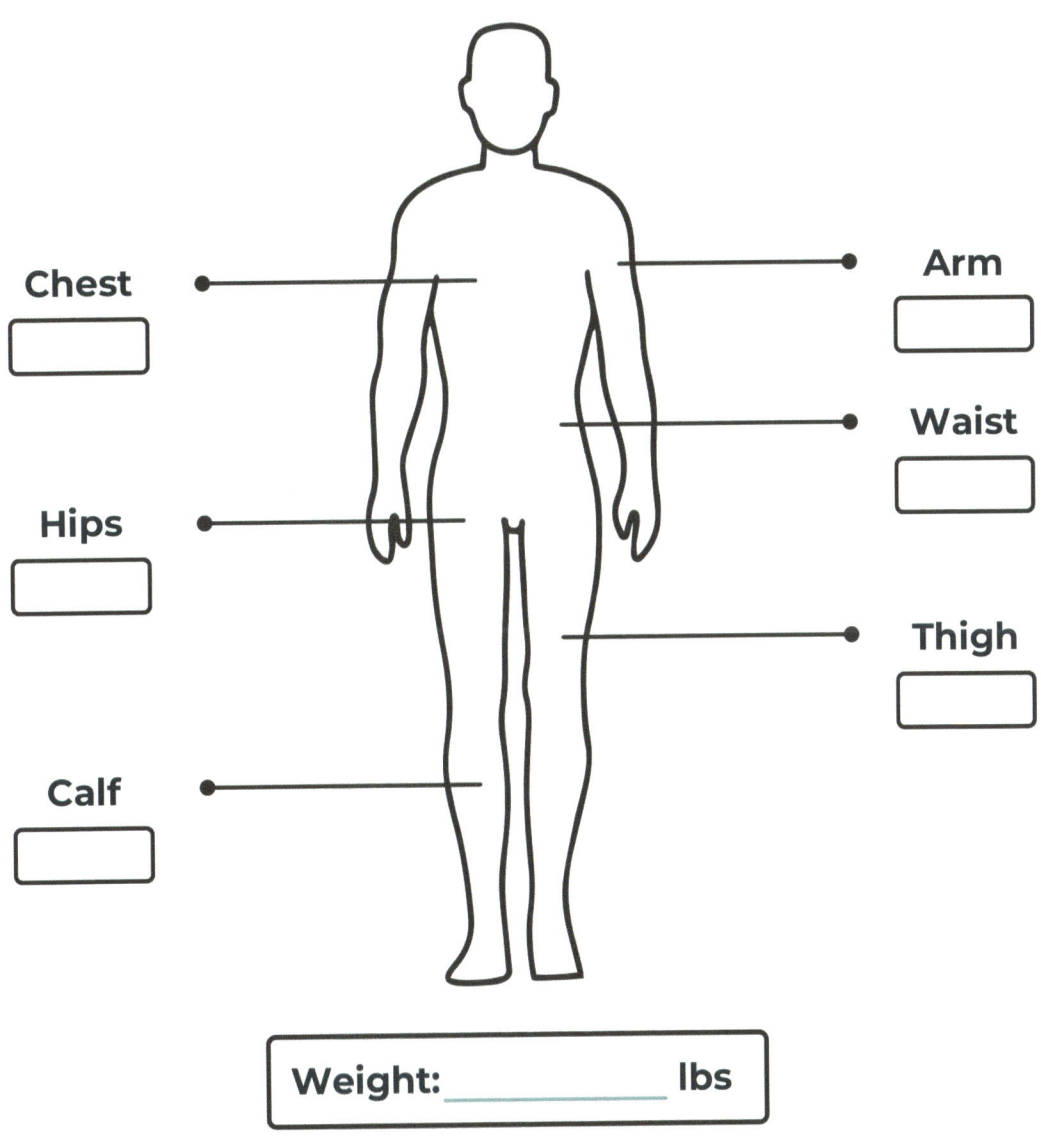

Chest

Arm

Hips

Waist

Calf

Thigh

Weight: _____ lbs

HOT SAUTÉED SALAD

This Hot Sautéed Three-Green Salad offers a tantalizing fusion of robust collard, mustard, and turnip greens, contrasted by the sweet tanginess of a tomato medley, the comfort of potatoes, and the smoky richness of turkey tails.

Recipe from the heart of
Arletha Kent

DIRECTIONS

1. **Prep**: Clean greens, slice tomatoes and dice potatoes.

2. **Preheat**: Simmer turkey tails in water (2 hours); save stock. Shred cooled meat.

3. **Sauté**: Cook onion and garlic in olive oil; add potatoes, seasoning, and cook. Combine tomatoes and chili pepper (if using) in the pan; sauté until softened.

4. **Cook Greens**: Toss in the greens, cover, and wilt (10 mins). Add turkey stock if needed.

5. **Add Turkey:** Add shredded turkey, and mix. Adjust seasoning and finish with lemon juice.

Enjoy this flavorful sautéed salad!

SERVINGS	PREP	COOKING
8	30 min	55-60 min

INGREDIENTS

- 1 bunch each of collard greens, mustard greens, and turnip greens
- 1 medley of tomatoes (varied colors if possible for visual appeal)
- 2 medium-sized potatoes
- 4 smoked turkey tails
- Salt, black pepper, garlic powder
- Olive oil
- 1 onion, finely chopped
- 2 cloves of garlic, minced
- 1 red chili pepper, deseeded and sliced (optional for some heat)
- Lemon juice for serving

"Overcoming obesity is more than weight loss; it's gaining a new perspective on life.

Diane White

SHELYNA TINGLIN
Entrepreneur | Author | Teacher | Coach

Meet Shelyna, a powerhouse taking on multiple roles as a devoted wife, mom, grandmother, and educator. With a career shift from teaching to real estate, she is now a licensed broker, author, speaker, trainer, mentor, and business coach.

As a Goldman Sachs 10,000 Small Business Program alumna and a member of Delta Sigma Theta Sorority, Inc., Shelyna is deeply rooted within her community. Her commitment to education shines through her master's degree in educational leadership and pursuit of a Ph.D. at the time this book was written.

Join her incredible journey, be inspired by her resilience, and let her show you how to unleash your true potential.

JAMAICAN BROWN STEW CHICKEN

"I had convinced myself that I was strong enough to handle it on my own and that I didn't need help."

INGREDIENTS

- Professional Support
- Self-Love
- Fellowship
- Personal Growth
- Protective Thoughts

Overcoming Past Trauma

DIRECTIONS

1. Seek professional help and support from therapists or counselors who specialize in trauma.

2. Practice self-love, such as exercising, healthy eating, meditation, and stress-reducing activities.

3. Build a support system of friends, family, and spiritual leaders.

4. Engage in activities that promote personal growth and self-discovery, such as journaling or creative arts.

5. Take hold of negative thoughts and change them by protecting your mind, heart, words, and actions.

My mother was 16 when she gave birth to me. She was slim, 5'5", with beautiful chocolate-smooth skin and no blemishes. I rarely remember her smile, but her teeth were so white. Her eyes were always slowly closing because of the drugs she was addicted to.

My father was tall with a muscular frame and deadly hands that he would use to beat others to a pulp or beat my mother in front of me. He was a part of the Brooklyn-born package, where anger and physical violence were the norm.

As a baby, my mother left me with her parents, who would later adopt me as their child; she didn't live to see 27. When I was 12, my mother was murdered after being thrown from the roof of a project building. I didn't feel any emotions but had one regret: not being able to say goodbye.

Trauma was a part of my DNA from birth. Rejection, judgment, abandonment, physical, emotional, and mental abuse, and constantly feeling like I didn't fit in. This affected how I interacted with people and the businesses I started, but I never connected them to trauma. I chopped it up to being a part of life.

Growing up in a black household taught you to just deal with your emotions and pray. No one ever stopped to think about my mental state or to get me the help and support I desperately needed.

As a child, dealing with trauma was difficult; it left me feeling unloved and vulnerable. I always felt like a burden and didn't know how to make friends. I adapted to others' personalities and spent money on them just to keep them from leaving me like my parents did.

My grandparents loved me, or they wouldn't have adopted me. Still, I felt rejected by the world and many other family members. I was always too dark or made fun of because my mother was strung out on drugs, or my father was in jail. I remember jumping rope in a park in Brooklyn, and she just sat there watching us.

It freaked everyone out, and when they asked if that was my mother, I said, "No, I don't know her!" I wanted friends so bad, people I could connect with, so I lied at the expense of disowning my mother.

I remember being taken from my grandmother's house to Connecticut without my 7-year-old opinion and becoming desperate for friends in this new place. I saw a girl outside playing whom I didn't know and decided I was going to be her friend.

So, one day, I went down to her house and rang the doorbell just as confident as I could be. I had a big smile because I knew I was about to make a new friend. The girl's mother came to the door and told her that I, one of her friends, had arrived. She saw me and told her mother she didn't know me, then slammed the door in my face.

I rode away, not fully understanding why she didn't want to be my friend, sad, and knowing that I would never try to be friends with a stranger again. That rejection felt just like what my parents had done to me. I was too young to process it then, but as I got older, I couldn't understand my hesitation to make friends, and it was connected to my feelings of hate and low sense of self-love.

I was broken without instructions to repair my mind and heart. It also put a block on growing my business because I was afraid of anything that would connect to someone telling me no, causing those feelings of rejection and abandonment to come back. I'd procrastinate because if it wasn't perfect, people would judge it and reject me.

Several other traumatic experiences shaped my life like being left alone at nine with my little brother – who was only five – in South Carolina after my parents were arrested for selling large amounts of drugs. The adult that was supposed to watch over us, whom we didn't know, left us.

My grandparents sent him money to send us back to New York but instead, he took the money and left us alone after a fistfight he had in front of us with some guy he was stealing computers with. I watched him walk down the street with his boom box and a bag over his shoulder, feeling abandoned again. Shortly after that, Hurricane Hugo hit. Nothing but God and His angels kept us alive in that home with no boarded-up windows, running water, or electricity. It sounded like a train was coming down the street, but I woke up to see an angel standing over us.

After Hugo passed, we were left alone with no adult to watch over us. If that wasn't bad enough, the children across the street from us, traumatized me and my brother, by setting my hair on fire and trying to molest me. We ended up locking ourselves in the abandoned home.

Fast forward to September 11, 2001. I was heading to a business meeting and escaped the Twin Towers falling by one train stop, running for my life from Manhattan to Brooklyn. My life flashed before my eyes as I ran, bumping into strangers, wondering if I would see my family again.

I started thinking back over my life - the physical, mental, and emotional abuse I endured that I couldn't stop. It brought a mixture of trauma and depression with regrets of never seeking help. My mind continued to spiral out of control for the next 20 years.

In the African American culture, you don't go to a therapist - you deal with life. You're also taught to have faith and pray to God about what you're going through. Yet, I was 41 years old, feeling like I would die if I didn't get help. My hands were shaking because I was embarking on a decision, I didn't want to make but knew I had to.

My anxiety was high, as I stood in the closet and sank to the floor, beginning the checkout process for my first consultation with a Christian therapist. As tears poured from my swollen eyes, my thoughts ran wild, telling me how embarrassing I was to my family for sharing our business with a stranger. I had to silence those thoughts and develop the courage to hit submit.

Reaching out for professional support from a therapist was the first step to gaining control of my thoughts and leaving trauma. For so long, I had convinced myself I was strong enough to handle it independently and didn't need help, but both were far from the truth. Through therapy, I had the support I needed and learned to cope with my triggers, face my fears and start a new foundation for my business by breaking down the walls that kept me bound.

Learning to love myself was not easy if you'd never been taught. It was a turning point for healing and forgiveness. Eating healthy, nourishing my mind with the Word of God, and my spirit with fellowship helped me to not revisit - and ease the strain of - my trauma.

Going for a walk and talking to God, meditating on scriptures around how I feel, and journaling allowed me to slow down and connect with my emotions, acknowledge the pain, and give myself permission to feel accepted and loved. The struggles may come when you are alone in your thoughts, but I want to encourage you to give it to God and change the thought the moment it enters your mind.

Let self-love become not just a statement but a practice. Be diligent about saying no and freeing yourself from the distractions of being busy. Focus on serving others through the skills and talents God has given you. Talk to a licensed therapist, fellowship, and break free from past trauma to have a productive life.

Overcoming Past Trauma

Inspired by Shelyna Tinglin's Journey

Note: This worksheet is designed to guide you through the process of overcoming trauma by drawing on the experiences of Shelyna Tinglin. Remember, it's a step toward healing, not an immediate solution.

Exercise 1: Acknowledging the Trauma
Reflect on your past experiences that have caused you trauma. Don't shy away from these memories; acknowledging them is the first step toward healing.

Write down some of your traumatic experiences below. Take your time and be as detailed as you feel comfortable.

_____
_____
_____
_____
_____
_____
_____
_____
_____
_____
_____
_____
_____
_____
_____
_____
_____
_____

Exercise 2: Identifying the Effects

Shelyna found her trauma affected not only her personal relationships, but also her business. How has trauma affected your life?

_____
_____
_____
_____

List the areas of your life where you see the effects of your past trauma. For example, friendships, work life, self-esteem, etc.

_____
_____
_____
_____

Exercise 3: Realizing the Need for Help

Shelyna recognized that she couldn't overcome her trauma alone. It's important to understand that reaching out for help isn't a sign of weakness.

Do you believe you can overcome your trauma alone or do you feel the need for professional help? Write down your thoughts.

_____
_____
_____
_____

Exercise 4: Seeking Professional Help

If you're ready, consider reaching out to a mental health professional. Therapists and psychologists can provide invaluable tools and strategies to manage and overcome trauma.

If you're considering seeking help, make a note of your fears or concerns. It might be helpful to discuss these with a potential therapist.

_____
_____
_____

Exercise 5: Self-Love and Acceptance

In her journey, Shelyna discovered the importance of self-love. She realized it wasn't just a statement but a practice that needed to be integrated into her life.

Write down five activities that make you feel happy, calm, or loved. Try to incorporate these into your daily routine.

_____

_____

_____

_____

Exercise 6: Healthy Habits

Shelyna nourished her body with healthy food and her spirit with fellowship. Consider how you can adapt your lifestyle to support your healing process.

What are some healthy habits you could adopt? They could be related to diet, exercise, spirituality, or social interactions.

_____

_____

_____

_____

Exercise 7: Mindfulness and Meditation

Shelyna found solace in prayer and scripture. Whether through faith or mindfulness practices, staying present can help alleviate the strain of past trauma.

Do you have mindfulness practice? If not, consider starting one. Write down some ideas.

_____

_____

_____

_____

Exercise 8: Identifying Triggers

Through therapy, Shelyna learned to identify and cope with her triggers. Recognizing what upsets, you can help you regain control.

Can you identify any of your triggers? Write them down and consider discussing them with a therapist or a trusted individual.

_____

_____

_____

_____

Exercise 9: Breaking Free

The ultimate goal is to break free from the effects of your past trauma. Shelyna managed to do this by focusing on her strengths and using them to serve others.

What are your strengths or talents? How can you use them to focus on a positive future and break away from past trauma?

_____

_____

_____

_____

Remember, it's okay to feel overwhelmed during this process. Take your time and remember to breathe. You're on the path to healing.

My Safety Plan

1 **My warning signs are:**

These could be specific thoughts, emotions, or actions that signify you might be at risk.

2 **My effective coping strategies are:**

These are activities that can boost your spirits, such as practicing mindfulness or engaging in physical exercise.

3 **Steps I can take to make my environment safer:**

Remember:
Help is only a call away

4 **People I can reach out to for distraction:**

5 People I can reach out to for help:

6 In the event of a crisis call:

Crisis Hotline

Emergency Contact

Emergency Services

You Are Your First Priority!

JAMAICAN BROWN STEW CHICKEN

Jamaican Brown Stew Chicken is a mouthwatering and iconic dish that captures the vibrant flavors of Jamaican cuisine. This is an easy version of Jamaican Brown Stew Chicken, filled with rich flavors, and perfect served with rice & peas, and cabbage.

Recipe from the heart of
Arletha Kent

DIRECTIONS

1. **Prep**: Marinate the chicken with salt, pepper, soy sauce, garlic, onion, and red pepper for 2 hours or overnight in the fridge.

2. **Make**:
   - Heat the sugar and oil in a pot until the sugar caramelizes.
   - Add the chicken (reserve the marinade) and brown it.
   - Add water, the reserved marinade, carrot, bell pepper, and thyme to the pot.
   - Simmer for about 40-50 minutes until the chicken is cooked and the stew is thick.

3. **Serve**: Stir in the green onions before serving.

   This simple Jamaican Brown Stew Chicken pairs perfectly with sides of rice, peas, and steamed cabbage. Enjoy!

SERVINGS	PREP	COOKING
4	15 min	1hr 15 min

INGREDIENTS

- 1 lb. chicken, cut into pieces
- Salt and pepper to taste
- 2 tbsps. soy sauce
- 2 cloves of garlic, minced
- 1 onion, chopped
- 1 hot pepper, chopped
- 1 tbsp. brown sugar
- 2 tbsps. oil
- 1 cup water
- 1 carrot, chopped
- 1 bell pepper, chopped
- 1 tsp. dried thyme
- 2 green onions, chopped

He who dwells in the secret place of the Most High shall abide under the shadow of the Almighty (Psalm 91:1).

Shelyna Tinglin

MICHAEL EVANS

Entrepreneur | Mentor | Author

Meet Michael, a transformational author and speaker who guides others toward self-discovery and healing. Born amidst family inconsistency, he journeyed from chaos to clarity, using his experiences to inspire resilience and change.

His book *Manniversary* chronicles his redemption from a turbulent past to a life marked by integrity, underpinned by faith. As a dedicated husband and father, Evans embodies the transformative power of commitment and personal growth, offering hope to others facing similar struggles.

STUFFED SPICY CHICKEN PEPPERS

"To no avail, the taste of women was a drug that drew me back into my indiscretions."

INGREDIENTS

- Honesty
- Compassion
- Self-restraint
- Commitment
- Consistency

Overcoming Sex Addiction

DIRECTIONS

1. Always tell the truth. Transparency is key!

2. Always consider how your decisions affect your significant other.

3. Temptations are always present, learn your triggers and don't put yourself in positions to compromise your integrity.

4. Create personal goals and honor them.

5. As human beings, we are forever evolving, seek creative ways to support and strengthen your personal and emotional development.

At the start of my journey, as far back as the age of 6, I faced a challenge that many young men encounter - an inconsistent father. His absence as a leader caused confusion and a mental shift in my life, making me turn to the atmosphere around me for guidance and to decompress situations. As a result, I experienced an identity crisis. Without proper household communication, I was in a downward spiral.

At the age of 13, we lost our home, which caused me significant resentment toward my father. I found solace in indulging in sexual tendencies that I truly enjoyed. I was always surrounded by associates who were cheaters, liars, and thieves. In high school I had poor work ethic, I did just enough to graduate, while still giving the sexual aspect of my life priority. However, I would eventually find myself spiraling out of control.

I couldn't help but think about the countless times my mother prayed for me during this time. She would take me to church, and although I would hear about God, Jesus, and the Holy Spirit, I didn't believe in their power to help me due to my destructive behavior. My life was a mess. I walked away from relationships repeatedly and blamed others for my mistakes.

By the age of 16, I hit rock bottom. I was deep into all the activities the streets had to offer, including a bullet with my name on it. But one day, I heard God's voice speak to me, reframing my perceptions about myself and life in general. He shared with me the 'two P's,' which I'll now share with you: purpose and position.

Purpose: He let me know there was something greater for me if I believed.

Position: He told me I could change the narrative. Each new day, I dictate my own reality.

This gave me the desire to be a better person. I made some necessary changes and even attempted to have a committed relationship. To no avail, the taste of women was a drug that drew me back into my indiscretions.

Between the ages of 17 and 28, I produced four children with no intentions of being a father, emulating my upbringing. While I was the type of dude that would buy clothes and shoes, I didn't understand how to bond with my kids. I was in and out, presently absent.

As time progressed, I failed to realize that I never wanted to be alone, not allowing myself to heal from the past hurts of my childhood. I hated being alone because, as a child, I always felt alone. So, I would jump from one bed into another. All the while, my heart was with my first child's mother.

We both were young with crazy family dynamics, which caused me to walk away from the relationship several times. I know now that was not the correct response. However, it was my only way to cope. I loved her so much, but we both had a lot of maturing to do. Eventually, I would work up the nerve to ask her to marry me, but she told me "NO!" She didn't trust me, and she had every right not to.

Just as I would when things didn't go as planned, I ran into another woman's arms, only validating why I wasn't ready for any relationship, especially marriage. After yet another failed attempt with that woman, I found myself back with my true love. This time we decided to try to fix our relationship. I asked her to marry me again, and this time she said, "YES!" With hard work and dedication, we pressed past our differences and said, "I DO!"

Ten years later, I found myself falling back into my old ways. Family issues influencing our relationship was a major factor in the conflict we were experiencing. Sure enough, I found comfort with another woman. Let's stick a pin right here.

This young lady and myself knew the Lord. Yet, we had the nerve to ask God to bless our relationship. He cracked both of our faces and told us to end it! I obeyed and ran back home. I sincerely apologized to my wife and re-committed to her, myself, and God. I found a church where I could learn His Word, learn how to be a better man, and intentionally create new habits and healthy practices to satisfy my sexual desires. I am proud to say that I have been faithful to my wife since that day.

I would be remiss to not give you an update on my father...our relationship has been restored. I'm proud of the man he has become, and I look forward to our relationship flourishing into what God intended it to be before the foundations of the world!

As you have followed me through my peaks and valleys, just know God loves you, no matter your struggles. It took me a while to understand the power and love of God. So, I share His Word that can keep you from falling. Learn from my mistakes, accept Jesus as your personal Lord and Savior, and you will overcome!

"No temptation has overtaken you except such as is common to man; but God is faithful, who will not allow you to be tempted beyond what you are able, but with the temptation will also make the way of escape, that you may be able to bear it."
1 Corinthians 10:13 NKJV

"Put on the whole armor of God, that you may be able to stand against the wiles of the devil. For we do not wrestle against flesh and blood, but against principalities, against powers, against the rulers of the darkness of this age, against spiritual hosts of wickedness in the heavenly places. Therefore take up the whole armor of God, that you may be able to withstand in the evil day, and having done all, to stand."
Ephesians 6:11–13 NKJV

Overcoming Addiction

Inspired by Michael Evans Journey

Exercise 1: Understanding Your Roots

Early Challenges: Just like Michael, reflect on your earliest memories and how they shaped you. Write down any challenges you faced growing up, especially those linked to parental figures and your household environment. Remember, this exercise is not to assign blame, but to understand your history and its impact on you.

_____
_____
_____
_____
_____
_____
_____
_____

Identity Crisis: Reflect on moments where you felt a loss of identity or confusion about who you were. What contributed to these feelings? Did you also seek external validation or guidance as Michael did?

_____
_____
_____
_____
_____
_____
_____
_____

Exercise 2: Acknowledging Your Struggles

Addictive Behavior: Identify and write down your addictive behaviors or dependencies, like Michael's struggle with sexual tendencies. What do you turn to for solace or escape?

_____
_____
_____
_____
_____
_____
_____
_____

Blame and Responsibility: Reflect on moments when you've blamed others for your mistakes or circumstances. Write them down and consider how taking responsibility might have changed the outcome.

_____
_____
_____
_____
_____
_____
_____
_____

Exercise 3: Finding Purpose and Position

Purpose: Michael found his purpose when he heard the voice of God. Reflect on your life purpose. What is something greater you believe is meant for you?

_____
_____
_____
_____
_____
_____
_____

Position: The concept of position is about changing your narrative and dictating your reality. What are some ways you can change your narrative starting today?

_____

_____

_____

_____

_____

_____

_____

_____

Exercise 4: Healing and Growing

The Past Hurts: Just like Michael never allowed himself to be alone to heal, identify if there are hurts from your past that you haven't addressed. Write down those hurts and how they might have influenced your addictive behavior.

_____

_____

_____

_____

_____

_____

_____

_____

Relationships: Reflect on your relationships, like Michael did with his first child's mother. Identify any patterns that might be contributing to your struggles. Consider what you can do differently to improve these relationships.

_____

_____

_____

_____

_____

Exercise 5: Commitment to Change

Recommitment: Just as Michael re-committed to his wife, himself, and God, take a moment to identify who or what you need to recommit to while overcoming your addiction.

_____
_____
_____
_____
_____
_____
_____
_____

New Habits: Michael learned how to be a better man and intentionally created new habits and healthy practices. What new habits can you start to replace your addictive behaviors?

_____
_____
_____
_____
_____
_____
_____
_____

Exercise 6: Acceptance and Faith

Acceptance: Reflect on your journey, acknowledge your mistakes, and accept them as a part of your growth. Write down the lessons you've learned from your mistakes.

_____
_____
_____
_____
_____
_____
_____

Faith: Like Michael, who leaned on his faith to overcome his struggles, identify a source of strength or faith you can turn to in times of temptation. How can this faith support you in overcoming your addiction?

_____

_____

_____

_____

_____

_____

_____

_____

Remember, the journey to overcoming addiction is not linear. It takes time, patience, and self-compassion. But by reflecting on your past, acknowledging your struggles, finding purpose, healing, recommitting, and leaning on faith, you can, just like Michael, overcome your addiction and create a healthier and happier future for yourself.

HABIT TRACKER

KEEPING TABS ON YOUR HABITS IS KEY TO MEETING YOUR GOALS. JOT DOWN YOUR TOP 12 AND GIVE YOURSELF A TICK EACH DAY YOU NAIL ONE. IT'S A DAILY HIGH-FIVE TO YOURSELF!

WEEK OF: _____

HABIT / SELF-CARE	S	M	T	W	T	F	S
01	○	○	○	○	○	○	○
02	○	○	○	○	○	○	○
03	○	○	○	○	○	○	○
04	○	○	○	○	○	○	○
05	○	○	○	○	○	○	○
06	○	○	○	○	○	○	○
07	○	○	○	○	○	○	○
08	○	○	○	○	○	○	○
09	○	○	○	○	○	○	○
10	○	○	○	○	○	○	○
11	○	○	○	○	○	○	○
12	○	○	○	○	○	○	○

REFLECTION NOTES

_____

_____

_____

_____

STUFFED SPICY CHICKEN PEPPERS

These Stuffed Spicy Chicken Peppers are a perfect fusion of succulent chicken, tangy bell peppers, and a hint of spice to ignite your taste buds.

Recipe from the heart of
Arletha Kent

DIRECTIONS

1. **Preheat**: Oven to 375°F.

2. **Prep**: Cut tops off peppers; scoop seeds.

3. **Sauté**: Cook onion and garlic in olive oil.

4. **Cook Chicken**: Add chicken; add seasoning.

5. **Mix & Fill**: Combine rice, cheese; then stuff peppers.

6. **Bake**: 30 mins at 375°F.

7. **Serve**: Cool, garnish, enjoy!

Enjoy these Stuffed Spicy Chicken Peppers as a healthy, flavorful main course for your next meal!

SERVINGS	PREP	COOKING
4	15 min	1hr 45 min

INGREDIENTS

- 4 large bell peppers
- 1 lb. ground chicken
- 1 large onion, finely chopped
- 2 cloves of garlic, minced
- 1 tbsp. olive oil
- 1 tsp. chili powder
- 1 tsp. cumin
- 1 cup of cooked rice
- 1 cup of shredded cheddar cheese
- Fresh parsley for garnish
- Salt and pepper; (Optional) Add any additional preferred seasonings

Always put God first!

Michael Evans

DALETTA LYNN

Author | Esthetician | Tax Professional

Meet Daletta the mastermind behind The Hazel Experience, a Texas-based fusion of beauty and financial services. As a skilled esthetician, she presents a superior hair removal solution for women that outlasts shaving by three to four weeks. Daletta's upbringing, marked by hardship, fuels her drive to break free from poverty. Passionate about empowering clients, her sought-after eBook delivers crucial money management insights.

She delivers comprehensive financial solutions as a licensed life insurance agent and tax preparer. Experience Daletta's uplifting journey as she triumphs over adversity and inspires us all.

SEAFOOD MEDLEY BOWL

"I vividly remember seeing bruises and scars, and it was a constant source of pain and sadness for me."

INGREDIENTS

- Diligence
- Endurance
- Discernment
- Self-Sufficiency
- Adaptability

Overcoming
The Loss of Innocence

DIRECTIONS

1. Seek counseling to learn your triggers to manage your emotions and avoid self-sabotage.

2. Diversify your social circle to experience new things.

3. Dive into personal development resources for inspiration and guidance to explore where you want to grow.

4. Cultivate independent thinking by being confident in your decisions.

5. Be determined to achieve every goal and fulfill every vision you believe God has given you!

My family and I moved to a small town called Duluth, Minnesota. That would ultimately become the birthplace of my new identity.

Having arrived in the middle of my ninth-grade year, I found myself in limbo, waiting nearly a month to begin school. This new environment, filled with strangers unaware of my past, presented a unique opportunity for reinvention.

However, as time passed, the previous 13 years of my life felt increasingly foreign. Desperate to hide my past, I became a chameleon, concealing my true self from those I had grown to know. Now, let's dive into what that old life was like and why I didn't want anyone to know about it.

My childhood memories are like a jigsaw puzzle that has missing pieces. I remember the constant moving - me, my mom, and my sister. We bounced around from relatives to friends, sometimes even shelters and motels. But it felt like a grand adventure, like we were exploring new worlds, even though we never really left the city.

Each new address felt like home, no matter who else was living there. The crazy thing is, I didn't even realize we were technically homeless. Who associates homelessness with being surrounded by friends and family, right?

We always called ourselves "Three the Hard Way." It was our way of saying that we were a team, and nothing could break us apart. No matter how bad things were, we got through it together.

My mother was a single parent, battling her own personal demons like unaddressed and unacknowledged childhood trauma. No one, including her own mother, believed in her trauma. She was being physically abused by her boyfriend, sometimes in front of us, and it affected the family dynamic. This contributed to the instability and financial challenges we experienced.

You know, there's a bunch of "normal" stuff I just can't remember – like the color of my room, my mom heading off to work, or if I ever had a real birthday party. But one thing I do remember is my mom giving me a chocolate cake every year on my birthday.

That cake was like this magical thing that made me feel seen and loved. It was like, at that moment, all the bad stuff faded away because it was my special day, and I was the birthday girl!

Although I have many happy memories from my childhood, filled with smiles and laughter, there were also times of fear and tears. I remember my mother and aunts being physically hurt and emotionally distraught. I vividly remember seeing bruises and scars, and it was a constant source of pain and sadness for me.

Among the families we lived with, there was a family with two boys around the same age as me and my sister. I don't remember how long we stayed with them, but I know that while living in that home, I experienced two of the most traumatic events of my life. These were some of the memories that I mentioned would drift in and out of my mind.

So, when I think back, I wonder if I was making it all up. Who would make up such messed-up memories, right? It wasn't until I was 28 and met this guy, who would be my future husband, that I started dealing with those memories.

We were having this deep chat one day, and suddenly, this memory hit me like a ton of bricks; I got all emotional. Tears were welling up, and the next thing I knew, I was spilling my guts to him. That's when it hit me. I'd never discussed that memory with anyone, not even my mom or sister.

Well, today, I'm sharing it with the world...I was sexually violated twice in this house, once by an adult male and once by the oldest boy. The first time I told my mother that the grown man touched me, she addressed the homeowners, and he was removed from the premises. Unfortunately, the police didn't get involved, but he was confronted by the family.

The second time, the boy lured me into his parents' room, where I ended up on the bed. As he assaulted me, I remember separating myself from the situation in my mind. I remember seeing the dresser on the right side of the bed, the wooden headboard, the old lady-patterned blanket, and the window. I couldn't wait for it to be over. When he was finished, I got up and quickly left the room to look for my sister. Besides my now-fiancé years later, this was never spoken of but also never forgotten.

Fast forward to 2004, and we left our last transitional housing and moved into a townhouse in Duluth, Minnesota. Now I'm surrounded by intact families. I listened to the friends I had made as they talked about the memories they shared from elementary school; The trips they went on with each other's families, even the school dances they went to together.

Everything I heard was things I saw in movies, and I couldn't relate. I would never contribute to those conversations, and when they asked, I would change the subject or make up a story.

I was experiencing both embarrassment and relief that my old life was a thing of the past. I was proud that "Three The Hard Way" made it to the other side. This was the year my mother left her abuser for good and put down alcohol. Life started to feel more stable than it had ever been before.

During my high school years, I was able to get involved in college prep programs and was part of multiple dance teams. My mom was able to build the life she dreamed of for us. Despite her challenges, my sister and I broke the cycle of poverty by finishing high school, growing up to have intact families with healthy relationships, and becoming business owners.

The best is yet to come!

Overcoming the Loss of Innocence

Inspired by Daletta Lynn's Journey

Exercise 1: Acknowledging Your Past

Your past, however painful, has played a pivotal role in shaping who you are today. Recognizing the truth of your experiences is the first step toward healing.

Write down some of the key events from your past that have shaped you. Don't judge them as good or bad, simply acknowledge them as parts of your life.

Example:
- Moving around from home to home with my family.
- Witnessing physical and emotional abuse.

_____

_____

_____

_____

Exercise 2: Facing the Trauma

The next step is acknowledging the traumatic events you've gone through. This is not an easy step but it's a necessary part of your healing journey.

List any traumatic events that you experienced in your past. Remember, it's okay to take a break if this task feels too overwhelming.

Example:
- Being sexually violated twice during my childhood.

_____

_____

_____

_____

Exercise 3: Breaking the Silence

Sometimes, the power of traumatic memories can be diminished by sharing them. By breaking the silence, you can begin to release the hold these experiences have on you.

Write a letter to a trusted person in your life, sharing a traumatic memory you've kept silent about. There is a blank page at the end of this exercise to write your letter. Remember, you don't have to actually send the letter unless you choose to.

Example:

Dear [Trusted Person],
I've held onto a painful memory from my past for far too long. It's time for me to share it...

_____

_____

_____

_____

Exercise 4: Building a New Identity

Having acknowledged your past, it's time to redefine who you are and who you want to be. This is your chance to create a new identity, independent of your past experiences.

Write down the characteristics of the person you aspire to become. What traits do they possess? What actions do they take?

Example:
- Confident
- Strong
- Trustworthy
- Successful business owner

_____

_____

_____

_____

Exercise 5: Cultivating Resilience

Just as Daletta and her family were "Three the Hard Way," resilience is a cornerstone of your journey. It is the ability to bounce back from adversity and keep moving forward.

Write down three times in your life when you showed resilience. What happened? How did you overcome the challenge?

Example:
- Despite the instability in my childhood, I finished high school and built a healthy family.
- Despite witnessing abuse, I created safe relationships in my life.
- Despite trauma, I found the courage to share my story.

_____

_____

_____

_____

Exercise 6: Envisioning Your Future

The future is yours to shape. Envisioning your future can provide motivation and hope as you continue your journey of healing.

Write a letter to your future self. What do you hope for? What advice can you give to your future self? There is a blank page at the end of this exercise to write your letter.

Example:

Dear Future Me,
I hope that you have become the person you aspired to be. I hope you've continued to show resilience and courage...

Step 7: Final Reflection

As you progress on this healing journey, regularly take time to reflect on your growth and transformation.

Write down three lessons you have learned through this healing journey.

Example:
- It's okay to acknowledge my past without being defined by it.
- Breaking my silence was a step.

_____

_____

_____

_____

Remember, every journey begins with a single step. As you reflect and work through this worksheet, you're taking important steps toward healing and reclaiming your story. There's a brighter future ahead of you, just like there was for Daletta.

SEAFOOD MEDLEY BOWL

Dive into our Seafood Bowl Medley, packed with tasty shrimp, sausage, and corn, sitting on a bed of rice. Seasoned with Old Bay, onion powder, garlic powder, and topped with parsley - it's a seaside feast in a bowl!

Recipe from the heart of
Arletha Kent

DIRECTIONS

1. **Prep:** Cook rice according to package instructions.

2. **Sauté:** Heat oil; cook onion, garlic, and sausages until browned (5-7 mins).

3. **Season & Cook Shrimp:** Sprinkle Old Bay, add shrimp; cook until pink (3-5 mins).

4. **Prepare Corn:** Boil corn until tender (5-7 mins), then add to the pan.

5. **Serve:** In individual bowls, place rice, top with the seafood mixture, and sprinkle with parsley.

Enjoy your delectable Seafood Medley Bowl, a blend of flavors that's sure to satisfy your cravings!!

SERVINGS	PREP	COOKING
4	15 min	30 min

INGREDIENTS

- 1 lb. shrimp
- 2 sausages, sliced
- 2 ears of corn, cut into rounds
- 2 tbsps. olive oil
- 1 small onion, chopped
- 2 cloves of garlic, minced
- 2 tsps. each of onion powder and garlic powder
- 2 tbsps. Old Bay seasoning
- Fresh parsley for garnish
- Cooked rice for serving

You have to get comfortable being uncomfortable, if you ever want to be successful.

Daletta Lynn

CHARLOTTE DOUGLAS

Financial Representative | Author | Mentor

Meet Charlotte, a resilient Independent Financial Representative, Author, and Mentor who believes in pursuing your dreams. Raised in a sheltered household, she navigated the challenges of growing up while lacking the social experiences of her peers.

Her journey through college, relationships, and unexpected detours taught her valuable lessons about self-discovery and the importance of making difficult choices. Now a successful professional and devoted single mother, Charlotte draws inspiration from her own experiences to guide others on their paths, instilling confidence, and the belief that it's never too late to achieve greatness.

HOMEMADE LASAGNA

"So, there I was, beautifully sheltered while being a bit naive and socially stagnant."

INGREDIENTS

- Transparency
- Foregivness
- Hope
- Perseverance
- Resilience

Overcoming a Sheltered Childhood

DIRECTIONS

1. Seek support and a safe space to share your feelings and experiences for guidance.

2. Forgive and release yourself from your past and learn from your mistakes.

3. Keep in mind, just as you made it through other things, this too shall pass.

4. Don't be distracted by your past by allowing it to exhaust you while working toward your future.

5. Keep trying, and never give up. Your next step will get you closer to your goal.

I genuinely believe that no matter where we come from or what mistakes we may make, it's never too late to reach our goals and dreams. We should never stop pushing ourselves to reach the next level If God didn't intend to help us along the way, He wouldn't have placed those aspirations within us.

My parents had four children: two boys and two girls. I was the second child and oldest girl, which carried a lot of responsibility and accountability. My oldest brother had the freedom that I could only imagine. In my household, boys could be boys, and the girls were protected.

Thinking back, my childhood and upbringing were awesome. I was blessed to have loving parents who were always there for us. I always felt secure, cherished, and incredibly sheltered! Of course, I know deep down that my parents did their absolute best in raising us, but let me tell you, the struggle was real!

In my family, we had this dynamic duo: my dad, the strong, ex-military figure, and my mom, the stay-at-home wife who took care of the home my dad provided for us. We had some awesome cousins, living in Chicago, and we had this cool tradition where we would take turns visiting each other during summer vacations. Those were always the best times, filled with fun and laughter.

One of my cousins came up with a nickname for our family-the Cunninghams – just like the ones from Happy Days. It struck me as funny, but I didn't fully grasp the meaning until much later. It turned out that the nickname referred to the roles we all played within our family.

Dad was the authoritative ex-military man, taking charge of things, while Mom was the caring nurturer. As for us kids, we knew the rules and stayed within the boundaries. So, there I was, beautifully sheltered while being a bit naive and socially stagnant.

I knew exactly what not to do, but as a young lady venturing out, I lacked the experience and direction to handle certain situations. Some conversations that were crucial never came up in my household. It was quite an interesting place to be. It was a constant struggle, knowing more about what not to do, to the extent that I learned about my menstrual cycle only after it arrived!

I did my best to navigate life, avoiding mistakes, and being the perfect kid. I ended up in public school and bumped up into 9th grade due to a technicality. There, among friends, I felt young and naive, realizing their maturity in handling sexual interactions left me feeling sheltered and inexperienced. I was unprepared for dealing with normal human tendencies and desires. The conversations they would have in gym class would really blow my mind.

Based on what my parents taught me, I couldn't help but think they were all going to hell. Also, let's not forget about the boys, who simply "get to be boys" without a second thought about the aftermath of their decisions.

I must admit, not everything was a complete disaster during my journey of growing up. I had some memorable moments, like experiencing my first kiss back in fifth grade and catching the attention of the new kid in class. And, of course, there was the Junior Prom! I actually went with the boy I had a crush on since fourth grade, and believe it or not, that crush lasted throughout junior high and all four years of high school.

But here's the thing, my feelings for him scared the living daylights out of me, so I never really tried to date him. The crush felt safer, you know? So, there I was, getting by with decent grades but still feeling socially handicapped. It was a balancing act, no doubt about it.

Fast forwarding to college, it was a new level of freedom! But real education happened outside the lecture halls. The student union and game room became my second home, and partying became a part of my college experience. I got so caught up in the social scene that I didn't quite make it to graduation.

Despite this, it wasn't all that bad. I always planned to go back to finish, but in the meantime, it was all about landing that "good" job. After my dad suggested the big three – electric, gas, and phone companies – at the age of 22, I ended up working at the phone company, and it felt like the jackpot. Finally, I moved out of my parent's place, sharing an apartment with my best friend and her son, living it up and keeping in touch with my college pals.

However, my mom assured me that if things didn't work out, I could always return home. When my roommate moved in with her fiancé, I did just that. I returned home briefly, but more adventures were waiting for me.

So, picture this: I'm at work, doing my thing, and minding my own business when suddenly, he strolls over to my workstation, and bam! Everything changes in an instant. Yep, that love bug bit me hard, and we started dating. I fell head over heels for this smooth, worldly, "alpha" male who knew how to take charge. Little did I know that beneath that charming exterior was a manipulative and controlling military-type guy. Sound familiar?

Well, let me tell you, our relationship had its fair share of difficulties. Despite my suspicion that he was being unfaithful, we were engaged not once but twice. I couldn't bring myself to say "I do" to a proposal that came with the side of uncertainty and the possibility of my future husband wanting to be with someone else.

After obtaining enough proof that he cheated on me, I called it quits. I found out I was pregnant during this time, and something inside me shifted. My mom, bless her heart, urged me to just go ahead and tie the knot to avoid having a baby out of wedlock, but deep down, I knew it wouldn't be the best situation for me or my child.

So, I made a tough decision. I said *no* to that sham of a proposal and decided to prioritize what was best for myself and my little one. It wasn't an easy path to take, but in the end, I knew it was the right choice.

There I was, unexpectedly finding myself on the path of single parenthood, something I swore I would never experience. It hit me like a ton of bricks, realizing that I, too, was just human and prone to making mistakes like everyone else. It was a tough pill to swallow, accepting that I wasn't as perfect as I thought I should be, especially coming from that seemingly flawless, God-fearing, and safe household I was raised in.

I had always believed that knowing what not to do would be enough to keep me on the right track. But boy, was I wrong. Consequently, my life turned out very different from the image of being married with children, holding a college degree, and having a great job.

It's incredible, though, how every detour, wrong turn, and unexpected road can still lead you to the place God has planned for you. It's a powerful realization that no matter the circumstances, there's always a divine plan waiting to unfold.

Through the roads I've traveled, I've gathered profound insights, mental toughness, and invaluable knowledge that have shaped me into who I am today. I'm proud to be an Independent Financial Representative, Author, and Mentor. But amidst all my accomplishments, one blessing stands above the rest: my child, a precious gift from God.

This incredible journey of parenthood has changed my perspective and broadened my vision, teaching me that it's alright to make mistakes and embrace my own humanity.

I've learned to grow through challenges, continuously move forward, and trust God's guidance. The responsibility of nurturing another life wasn't easy. Still, with God's grace, I've provided a sheltered environment while encouraging open communication, teaching right from wrong, and fostering confidence and growth.

My child has achieved so much, driven by her own aspirations and dreams, knowing that she can reach her goals with unwavering determination. It's a remarkable journey of faith, growth, and the profound impact of God's guidance in our lives.

Overcoming A Sheltered Childhood

Inspired by Charlotte Douglas' Journey

Exercise 1: Identifying Unfulfilled Needs

Accept your background: Recognize your upbringing for what it was–protective, secure, and well-intended, but also recognize its limitations. How did it affect your growth and social experiences? Write down some examples here:

_____

_____

_____

_____

Exercise 2: Confront Your Fears

Often, a sheltered upbringing can lead to feelings of fear and discomfort when facing unfamiliar situations. List some situations that you find difficult to navigate due to your background:

_____

_____

_____

_____

Exercise 3: Seek New Experiences

Actively engage in different activities, meet diverse people, and expose yourself to new ideas. Write down some ways you could broaden your horizons:

_____

_____

_____

_____

Exercise 4: Reevaluate Your Beliefs

Like Charlotte, you might have had preconceived notions about what is "right" or "wrong," due to your upbringing. Take the time to question these beliefs and form your own opinions. Write down some beliefs you'd like to re-evaluate:

_____

_____

_____

_____

Exercise 5: Embrace Your Humanity

Accept that it's okay to make mistakes. Reflect on past errors you've made and how you've grown from them:

_____

_____

_____

_____

Exercise 6: Chart Your Own Path

Despite what your parents/guardians may have envisioned for you, remember that your life is your own. Write down your dreams and goals:

_____

_____

_____

_____

Exercise 7: Trust in Divine Guidance

Just as Charlotte did, learn to trust that there is a divine plan for you, even when things seem challenging or confusing. Reflect on moments in your life when things fell into place in unexpected ways:

_____

_____

_____

_____

Exercise 8: Take the Next Step

What are some concrete actions you can take to move forward? List them below:

_____

_____

_____

_____

Remember Charlotte's key message: No matter where we come from or what mistakes we may make, it's never too late to reach our goals and dreams. We should never stop pushing ourselves to reach the next level. This belief was instrumental in Charlotte's journey from a sheltered girl to an accomplished woman, and it can guide your journey, too.

SMART
GOALS

WHEN IT'S TIME TO SET YOUR GOALS, LET'S MAKE THEM SMART. USE THE FOLLOWING QUESTIONS AS A GUIDE TO SHAPE YOUR AMBITIONS. YOU'VE GOT THIS!

| **S** | **SPECIFIC**
WHAT DO I WANT TO ACCOMPLISH? | |

| **M** | **MEASURABLE**
HOW WILL I KNOW WHEN IT IS ACCOMPLISHED? | |

| **A** | **ACHIEVABLE**
HOW CAN THE GOAL BE ACCOMPLISHED? | |

| **R** | **RELEVANT**
DOES THIS SEEM WORTHWHILE? | |

| **T** | **TIME BOUND**
WHEN CAN I ACCOMPLISH THIS GOAL? | |

HOMEMADE LASAGNA

An effortless lasagna recipe filled with ground beef, cheddar cheese, and a simple tomato sauce, creating a comforting and delicious dinner.

SERVINGS	PREP	COOKING
6	20 min	1hr 20 min

INGREDIENTS

- 1 tbsp. oil
- 1 onion, chopped
- 1 green pepper, chopped
- 2 cloves of garlic, minced
- (Optional) Add cilantro, basil, or parsley
- 1 lbs ground beef
- 24 oz. of marinara sauce
- 1/2 cup of sugar
- Salt, pepper and other seasoning of your choice to taste
- 9 lasagna noodles
- 3-4 cups shredded cheese of choice (4 variations are recommended)

Recipe from the heart of:
Arletha Kent

DIRECTIONS

1. **Prep**: Cook the lasagna noodles according to package instructions; drain and set aside.

2. **Sauté**: In a large skillet, cook ground beef, onion, green pepper and garlic over medium heat until browned. Drain excess fat.

3. **Brown Beef & Simmer Sauce**: Stir in marinara sauce, seasonings of choice, sugar, basil, salt, black pepper, and parsley. Simmer for about 30 minutes. (Season to taste)

4. Preheat oven to 375°F.

5. **Layer Lasagna**: Spread a thin layer of the meat sauce in the bottom of a 9x13-inch baking dish.

- Layer with 3 cooked lasagna noodles, meat, and cheese.

- Repeat layers and top with the remaining meat sauce and cheese.

6. **Cover with Aluminum Foil** and bake in the preheated oven for 25 minutes.

7. **Remove the Foil and Bake** for an additional 25 minutes, until bubbly and golden.

"

No matter where we come from or what mistakes we may make it's never too late to reach our goals and dreams.

Charlotte Douglas

THANK YOU!

We are truly thankful that you, dear reader, have accompanied us on this incredible journey. Your presence has enriched this shared experience, adding depth and warmth to every page. We hope you've found both inspiration and comfort within these pages, seeing them as a reflection of your strength and resilience.

May these stories, recipes, and resources satisfy your appetite and fortify your spirit, enabling you to conquer whatever challenges life may serve. We're grateful to have been part of your journey and can't wait to hear about the victories you will undoubtedly achieve. From the bottom of our hearts, thank you. Keep shining, keep striving, and above all, keep believing. God bless!

Arletha Kent

PROFESSIONAL SUPPORT

IMPORTANT NOTICE: RESOURCES AND SUPPORT

The Literary Lighthouse Alliance wishes to emphasize that it is not affiliated with any of the resources mentioned below. As readers from different corners of the world, we strive to share reputable, nationally available resources that you can rely on. Our goal is to support you and provide information that can assist you in finding the help you need.

DISCLAIMER:

The Literary Lighthouse Alliance is not responsible for the content or services provided by the mentioned resources. The resources listed on this page are current as of June 12, 2023. The information presented is for informational purposes only. For the most accurate and updated details, please contact the relevant resources directly.

HOTLINE SUPPORT: A LIFELINE

The hotlines provided are a lifeline, my friend. They are manned by compassionate professionals trained to lend a helping hand, offer support, and guide you through tough times. The best part is that they are available around the clock, ready to listen and provide confidential services. Knowing that help is just a phone call or text message away can be incredibly reassuring, regardless of the challenges you may be facing.

LIMITATIONS AND EMERGENCY SITUATIONS:

However, it is crucial to remember that while these hotlines offer invaluable support, they cannot replace professional medical or psychological advice. If you or someone you know is in immediate danger or facing a life-threatening emergency, please reach out to your local emergency services without delay. They are equipped to handle such situations and provide immediate assistance.

YOU MATTER: SEEKING HELP AND HEALING

Remember, you matter, my friend. Your well-being is incredibly important, and you should never hesitate to seek help when you need it. It takes strength to ask for support, and by reaching out, you are taking a crucial step towards healing. Always remember, hope and brighter days are waiting for you!

BLESS YOU AND TAKE CARE:

Bless you, my friend! Take care of yourself and know that there are people who genuinely care about your well-being.

Resources
LIFE LINES ~ PROFESSIONAL SUPPORT

LGBTQ+ National Help Center:
Hotline: 1-888-843-4564
Website: gaycenter.org

Veterans Crisis Line:
Hotline: 988 (Press option 1)
Website: veteranscrisisline.net

Trans Lifeline:
Hotline: 1-877-565-8860
Website: translifeline.org

Crisis Text Line:
Text "Home" to 741741
(US and Canada)
Website: crisistextline.org

National Parent Helpline:
Hotline: 1-855-427-2736
Website: nationalparenthelpline.org

Resources

LIFE LINES ~ PROFESSIONAL SUPPORT

National Teen Dating Abuse Helpline:
Hotline: 1-866-331-9474
Website: youth.gov

National Suicide Prevention Lifeline:
Hotline: 988 (Press option 1)
Website: suicidepreventionlifeline.org

National Human Trafficking Hotline:
Hotline: 1-888-373-7888
Website: humantraffickinghotline.org

National Sexual Assault Hotline:
Hotline: 1-800-656-HOPE
(1-800-656-4673)
Website: rainn.org

National Domestic Violence Hotline:
Hotline: 1-800-799-SAFE
 (1-800-799-7233)
Website: thehotline.org

Resources

LIFE LINES ~ PROFESSIONAL SUPPORT

 **National Helpline for Substance Abuse and Mental Health Services:**
Hotline: 1-800-662-HELP
(1-800-662-4357)
Website: samhsa.gov

 **National Council on Problem Gambling Helpline:**
Hotline: 1-800-GAMBLER
(1-800-426-2537)
Website: ncpgambling.org

 **National Eating Disorders Association Helpline:**
Business Phone Number: 212-575-6200
Website: nationaleatingdisorders.org

 **National Alliance to End Homelessness Helpline:**
Hotline: 1-800-548-6598
Website: endhomelessness.org

 **National Alliance on Mental Illness (NAMI) Helpline:**
Hotline: 1-800-950-NAMI
(1-800-950-6264)
Website: nami.org

Resources

National Runaway Safeline:
Hotline: 1-800-RUNAWAY
(1-800-786-2929)
Website: 1800runaway.org

National Child Abuse Hotline:
Hotline: 1-800-4-A-CHILD
(1-800-422-4453)
Website: childhelphotline.org

National Grief Support Hotline:
Hotline: 988 (Press option 1)
Website: 988lifeline.org

Emerald Stars of Support

THE LITERARY LIGHTHOUSE ALLIANCE

- Service: Literary Services/Publishing
- Website: theliterarylighthousealliance.com
- CEO: Arletha Kent

TINGLIN COACHING & CONSULTING

- Service: Real Estate Broker, Trainer, Speaker
- Website: coach.shelynatinglin.com
- CEO: Shelyna Tinglin

A NEW ME COUNSELING & CONSULTING

- Service: Counseling, Life Coaching, & Consulting
- Website: anewmedre.com
- CEO: Dr. Estrelita Bruce

POPE FINANCIAL SOLUTIONS

- Service: Innovative Financial Solutions
- Website: popefinancial.net
- CEO: NaTosha Pope

Emerald Stars of Support

FREESTYLE SWITCH DESIGNZ

- Service: Graphic Design
- Website: esty.com/shop/FreestyleSwitch
- Co-CEO: Fredericka Lartey

KADENA TATE

- Service: Revenue Strategist
- Website: kadenatate.com
- CEO: Kadena Tate

ONPOINTE ALLIANCE

- Service: Fingerprinting & Training
- Website: onpointealliance.com
- CEO: Arletha Kent

Gold Stars of Support

MICHEL HAMBRICK AGENCY

- Service: Insurance
- Website: michelhambrickinsurance.com
- CEO: Michel Hambrick

VARIABLE PROFESSIONAL SOLUTIONS

- Service: On-Line Notary
- Website: variableprofessionalsolutions.com
- CEO: Rabiah Hogans

GROWING THROUGH LIFE INTERNATIONAL

- Service: Holistic Coaching & Consulting
- Website: growingthroughlife.net
- CEO: Dr. Aundrea T. Harris

MUSIC GATES FULL SERVICE ENTERTAINMENT

- Service: One-Stop Shop For Audio & Visual
- Contact: info@musicgatesent.org
- CEO: Mahkya Askew

Gold Stars of Support

FAITH CONNECTION

- Service: Holistic Counseling & Online Store
- Website: AFaithConnection.com
- CEO: Dr. Aundrea T. Harris

J WILLIS PRODUCTIONS

- Service: Audio & Visual Production
- Website: visionofj.org
- CEO: J Willis

A. L. BEAN & COMPANY

A.L. BEAN & COMPANY

- Service: Consulting, Tax & Accounting
- Website: albeancompany.com
- CEO: Art Bean

FREEZING TIPS

Arletha has learned a lot about freezing food from her time in the kitchen and she wants to share some valuable tips with you.

- Freeze foods in portions.
- Seal the food using plastic wrap, freezer bags or plastic containers to keep moisture out.
- Label all sealed food with the type of food and date it was made.
- After thawing previously frozen food, only refreeze it once it has been cooked.
- If in doubt, throw it out. Freezing doesn't kill bacteria so if you're wary when something has defrosted, don't use it.

FOOD	TIME	NOTES
Whole chicken	1 year	Wrap well
Roasting meat cuts (beef, lamb)	9 - 12 mo	
Chops and steaks	6 - 9 mo	
Chicken pieces (breast, thigh, leg)	6 - 9 mo	
Oily fish fillets (salmon, mackerel)	2 - 3 mo	
White fish fillets (cod, haddock)	6 mo	
Chillies, ginger (whole)	6 mo	Grate or chop while frozen
Nuts	1 year	
Butter	6 mo	
Cheese - (Cheddar, Mozzarella, Gouda)	3 mo	Grated cheese can be used frozen
Eggs	3 - 6 mo	Beaten in a container, not in shell
Milk	6 mo	
Bananas	6 mo	
Berries	3 mo	
Blanched vegetables	1 year	
Cooked meals / soups	3 mo	
Cakes (un-iced)	3 mo	Defrost unwrapped
Bread (loaf, slices, pitta)	3 mo	Defrost slices in the toaster

RECIPE TESTING

RECIPE	RATING
	☆☆☆☆☆
	☆☆☆☆☆
	☆☆☆☆☆
	☆☆☆☆☆
	☆☆☆☆☆
	☆☆☆☆☆
	☆☆☆☆☆
	☆☆☆☆☆

NOTES:

_____

_____

_____

GROCERY LIST

FRUITS AND VEGETABLES

_____   _____
_____   _____
_____   _____
_____   _____

MEAT AND FISH

_____   _____
_____   _____
_____   _____
_____   _____

CANNED GOODS

_____   _____
_____   _____
_____   _____
_____   _____

BREAD/PASTA/GRAINS

_____   _____
_____   _____
_____   _____
_____   _____

SNACKS

_____   _____
_____   _____
_____   _____

DAIRY AND EGGS

_____   _____
_____   _____
_____   _____
_____   _____

FROZEN

_____   _____
_____   _____
_____   _____
_____   _____

BEVERAGES

_____   _____
_____   _____
_____   _____
_____   _____

BAKING

_____   _____
_____   _____
_____   _____
_____   _____

OTHER

_____   _____
_____   _____
_____   _____

GROCERY LIST

FRUITS AND VEGETABLES

_____ _____
_____ _____
_____ _____
_____ _____

DAIRY AND EGGS

_____ _____
_____ _____
_____ _____
_____ _____

MEAT AND FISH

_____ _____
_____ _____
_____ _____
_____ _____

FROZEN

_____ _____
_____ _____
_____ _____
_____ _____

CANNED GOODS

_____ _____
_____ _____
_____ _____
_____ _____

BEVERAGES

_____ _____
_____ _____
_____ _____
_____ _____

BREAD/PASTA/GRAINS

_____ _____
_____ _____
_____ _____
_____ _____

BAKING

_____ _____
_____ _____
_____ _____
_____ _____

SNACKS

_____ _____
_____ _____
_____ _____

OTHER

_____ _____
_____ _____
_____ _____

Behind The Scenes

Enjoy the behind the scenes of our photoshoots...
We all had a blast!
Our collaborators worked together from the following States:

~MISSOURI~

Diane White
Charlotte Douglas

~NEW JERSEY~

Rabiah Hogans

~TEXAS~

Michael Evans
Daletta Lynn
Shelyna Tinglin
Travis C. Kent Jr
Arletha Kent

The Secret Recipes
of an *Overcomer*

"How to transition from Defeat to Victory"

ARLETHA KENT
7 LITERARY COLLABORATORS

THE LITERARY LIGHTHOUSE
ALLIANCE

VISIONARY:
ARLETHA KENT &
COHORT #1 - 2023